Pass the Poetry, Please!

Using Poetry in Pre-Kindergarten-Six Classrooms

Lee Bennett Hopkins
Curriculum and Editorial Specialist
Scholastic Magazines, Inc.

CITATION PRESS   NEW YORK   1972

For reprint permission, grateful acknowledgment is made to:

Harcourt Brace Jovanovich, Inc. for "Keep a Poem in Your Pocket" by Beatrice Schenk de Regniers from *Something Special,* copyright © 1958, by Beatrice Schenk de Regniers.

J. B. Lippincott Company for "Poetry" by Eleanor Farjeon, copyright 1938 by Eleanor Farjeon, renewal, © 1966 by Gervaise Farjeon. From the book *Poems for Children* by Eleanor Farjeon, Copyright, 1951, by Eleanor Farjeon.

Scholastic Magazines, Inc. for a concrete poem from *The Laugh Book* by Ruth Belov Gross, pictures by Leslie Jacobs, copyright © 1971 by Ruth Belov Gross.

Thanks—To Misha Arenstein who listened, to Charles J. Egita who helped, to the many people in publishing who shared, and to Mary L. Allison who believed.

—Lee Bennett Hopkins

To my poet-friends
who make it all possible
LBH

Other Citation Press Books by Lee Bennett Hopkins

LET THEM BE THEMSELVES
Language Arts Enrichment for Disadvantaged Children in
Elementary Schools   1969

BOOKS ARE BY PEOPLE
Interviews with 104 Authors and Illustrators of Books for
Young Children   1969

PARTNERS IN LEARNING
A Child-Centered Approach to Teaching the Social Studies
(with Misha Arenstein)   1971

A CHILDREN'S LITERATURE KIT
A Balanced Collection for Teachers and Students Pre-K–3
                                                      1972

Pass the Poetry, Please!

CONTENTS

POETRY IS MANY THINGS

AN INTRODUCTION

Children are natural poets. Visit a school playground or park on a spring day and you will see youngsters "rhyming." Three girls playing jump rope might be exclaiming:

Grace, Grace, dressed in lace
Went upstairs to powder her face.
How many boxes does she use
One, two, three, four...

until one misses and either this rhyme or another is recited for the next jumper. Another group of children beginning a game of hide-and-go-seek or tag may be deciding who is going to be "it" by chanting:

Eenie, meenie, minee, mo,
Catch a tiger by the toe.
If he hollers, let him go,
Eenie, meenie, minee, mo.

My mother and your mother were
hanging out clothes.
My mother punched your mother
right in the nose.
What color blood came out?
R-E-D spells *red* and O-U-T spells *out*.

Still other groups of girls and boys will be bouncing balls and calling out:

A sailing sailor
Went to sea
To see what he could see, see, see.
And all that he could see, see, see
Was the sea, the sea
The sea, sea, sea.

Children make up their own rhymes at play, too:

Booba, booba, baba, baba,
Twee, twee, toe, toe
I know, I know!

Rhyme is very present in the child's world.

Over the years I have listened long and hard to girls and boys. My work has taken me across the United States, and I have encountered children in a variety of formal and informal situations. Sharing poetry has always been, and always will be, one of the greatest satisfactions of my life. In the early grades I have seen children naturally *ooh* and *ah* when they heard a poem they liked; I have also seen them wince and screw up their faces when a poem did not please them.

In upper grades where I have worked, poetry served as an excellent stimulus to better reading and nurtured a love of words. I have used poetry with slow readers in my classes—readers who could not possibly get through a long story but who could understand the message a poem contains. Poems, being short, are not demanding or frustrating to these readers. They can start them, finish them, and gain from them without experiencing any discomfort whatsoever.

Many children in the upper grades, whether slow readers or very good readers, may not be mature enough to tackle the sophisticated prose work of some of America's men of letters, but they can dip into the poetry of the very best; they can easily read and understand poems by such masters as Carl Sandburg, Robert Frost, and Langston Hughes. Thus, children's literary horizons can be extended through verses created by some of the finest writers.

Children in the elementary grades are not much different from most adults when it comes to knowing and/or loving poetry. They have their definite tastes just as adults do. The reason is that poetry is many things to many people. There have been many classic definitions of poetry. For instance, the anthologist Gerald D. McDonald has stated in his book *A Way of Knowing* (T. Y. Crowell, 1959, p. xi):

Poetry can be wittier and funnier than any kind of writing; it can tell us about the world through words we can't forget; it can be tough or it can be tender, it can be fat or lean; it can preach a short sermon or give us a long thought (the shorter the poem sometimes, the longer the thought). And it does all this through the music of words.

The poet David McCord commented to me (*Books Are by People,* Citation Press 1969, p. 169):

Poetry is so many things besides the shiver down the spine. It is a new day lying on an unknown doorstep. It is *Peer Gynt* and *Moby Dick* in a single line. It is the best translation of words that do not exist. It is hot coffee dripping from an icicle. It is the accident involving sudden life. It is the calculus of the imagination. It is the finishing touch to what one could not finish. It is a hundred things as unexplainable as all our foolish explanations.

A poem is an experience—something that has happened to a person, something that may seem very obvious, an everyday occurrence that has been set down in a minimum number of words and lines as it has never been set down before. These experiences depend upon the poet: who he is, when and where he lives, why and how a specific thing affected him at a given moment.

In an eulogy to William Carlos Williams, the poet John Ciardi wrote (*Saturday Review,* March 23, 1963, p. 18):

A good poem celebrates life and quickens us to it. . . . The good poet cannot fail to shame us, for he proves to us instantly that we have never learned to touch, smell, taste, hear, and see. He shames us through our senses by awakening us to a new awareness of the peaks and abysses locked in every commonplace thing.

But he shames us with such joy that the sensations of joy are lost in the delight of our awakening. We realize, exalted, that the good poet stirs us to an energy of being that we could not have known by ourselves, and we grow to love him in gratitude and joy. His gift of life is in his power to shape his experiences—and thereby to live them—in an ardor of sensation and energy beyond our daily reach. But beyond it only until he quickens and extends us to his higher power.

There are as many definitions of poetry as there are poets; their works reflect this diversity, enabling us to choose from a myriad of poems.

Life has produced poets who need the quiet of the country, and they share what their senses reveal. For many the sight of a brook, a reflection in a pond, or "a host of daffodils" inspires fresh images of nature. But recently new voices are creating poetry—poets who are immersed in the urban environment and who write poems about city experiences. Nancy Larrick, in her introduction to *On City Streets* (M. Evans, 1968; also available in paperback from Bantam), comments on this new trend:

For many years children's poets wrote only sweet gentle songs of country life. Anthologists compiling for young readers selected poems about fragrant hay and pumpkin vines . . .

But today most Americans live in the city, and even those in small towns and rural areas are just as urbanized as their city cousins, thanks to television. Rural children in a school bus can tell you more about the bus and the traffic lights than flowers along the country road.

No matter where and when poets live, or where and when they write poetry, all poets write of everyday happenings from their own point of view, about their environment.

The article "From a Different Point of View" by Ellen King (Scholastic's *NewsTime,* April 5, 1971) pinpoints this idea by examining three themes: *The City* contrasts William Wordsworth's "Upon Westminster Bridge" to the contemporary poem "The Telephone" by Edward Field; *Identity* contrasts Emily Dickinson's classic poem beginning "I'm nobody! / Who are you?" to Langston Hughes' "I, Too"; *Freedom* contrasts "Freedom's Symphony" by John Okai, a poet from Ghana, Africa, to "On an Alaskan Fur Farm" by the Russian, Yevgeny Yevtushenko. This type of article, written specifically for children, starts them thinking and shows them how different people's feelings and thoughts are expressed in poetry.

Life itself is embodied in poetry, and each poem reveals a bit of life. Good poems make us sigh and say, "Yes, that's just how it is." Or, as Carl Sandburg wrote in his "Tentative Definitions of Poetry" printed as the preface to *Good Morning, America* (Harcourt, 1928, 1956): "Poetry is the report of a nuance between two moments when people say, 'Listen!' and 'Did you see it?' 'Did you hear it? What was it?'"

There is really little difference between good poetry for children and adults. Poetry for children should appeal to them— meet their emotional needs and interests. By excepting this criteria, the world of poetry opens up for everyone. Teachers can read about what poetry or a poem *is,* what they *should* do, learn all about meters, rhyme schemes, cadence, and balance; yet all this does not necessarily help to make a poem meaningful. The one criteria we must set for ourselves is that we like—nearly love—the poems we read and are going to share. If we don't like a particular poem, we shouldn't read it; our distaste will certainly show to the children. There are plenty of poems around. Why bother with those that are not pleasing? In the world of poetry almost anything can work.

People's eyes have flashed at the idea of presenting poetry by such greats as e. e. cummings, Theodore Roethke, or Wallace Stevens to children in elementary grades, yet it can and has been done successfully. I uppose that once brows were also raised at the thought of bringing "adult literature" into the elementary school—books such as *20,000 Leagues Under the Sea* or *Gulliver's Travels*. We all know that these novels have proved to be popular with children. The language and thoughts of poetry written primarily for adult audiences can also appeal to young girls and boys.

Renée Karol Weiss proved this when she put together the handsome anthology *A Paper Zoo: A Collection of Animal Poems by Modern Americans* (Macmillan, 1968). While teaching kindergarten in a public school in a small poor town, Mrs. Weiss used poems by William Carlos Williams, Theodore Roethke, and e. e. cummings, "because young children, in their usual encounters with poetry, are unlikely to meet them, and because contemporary language speaks directly to the child." Thus, the words of these poets echoed in her room along with nursery rhymes.

When Misha Arenstein and I compiled the anthology *Faces and Places: Poems for You* (Scholastic Book Services, 1971) we carefully selected works that would especially appeal to children in upper elementary grades. Mr. Arenstein, an elementary teacher in the Edgemont School District (Scarsdale, New York), read, re-read, and sought reactions from his class to each of the poems in the anthology. The children responded equally well to T. S. Eliot's, "Macavity: the Mystery Cat," Langston Hughes' "Mother to Son," and ancient haiku as they did to poems written "for children" such as Harry Behn's "Adventure," Myra Cohn Livingston's "This Thing Called Space," and Gwendolyn Brooks' "Jim."

While working with boys and girls across the country I have always read a balance of the old and new, poems written "for adults," poems written "for children," and often poems written by children for children.

Many classroom teachers may not want to read "sophisticated" poetry to children, particularly if the poetry is somewhat strange to them. Some teachers may never feel comfortable reading to children in primary, or even upper grades, such selections as T. S. Eliot's "The Naming of Cats"; this poem does have difficult pacing and hard-to-read phrases such as "...rapt contemplation" and "...ineffable effable/Effanineffable/Deep and inscrutable singular Name."

Because this particular poem worked for Mrs. Weiss and for me, it doesn't mean it will work for you. You know your children and their tastes, and, moreover, you know what appeals to you! Stay comfortable. If "The Naming of Cats" doesn't please you, look for another cat poem. You'll find many: "Cat" by Eleanor Farjeon is filled with many good sound words such as *pftts, spitch* and *spatch,* and John Ciardi's "My Cat, Mrs. Lick A Chin," a cat who "Never knows where she *wants* to be," are two examples.

The anthologists Sara and John E. Brewton have prepared an *Index to Children's Poetry: A Title, Subject, Author, and First Line Index to Poetry to Collections for Children and Youth,* (H. W. Wilson, 1942, plus three supplements). In this volume you can find listed well over one hundred cat poems, and if *dogs* are your favorites, you can find over one hundred poems listed about them in the *Index* too!

7

Bringing children and poetry together can be one of the most exciting experiences in a teaching career. Two of the reasons teachers infrequently use poetry with children are that many of them are either afraid of it or they were turned off during their own school years by the mere mention of the word *poetry*.

I well remember hating Shakespeare as a high school student. I was forced to memorize and analyze some fifteen lines from *Julius Caesar*. The class had a written and an oral test on the "Friends, Romans, countrymen..." speech. I received an A on the oral but a C on the written test because I misspelled several words and left out some punctuation marks! The next semester I suffered through a similar experience with Alfred Noyes' "The Highwayman." I, too, soon came to detest the sound of the word poetry. It was not something to be enjoyed —it was a test of endurance and memorization ability.

Looking back on my own high school days I laugh now, but I still wonder why girls and boys have to suffer through poetry presented in such a dreary, uninteresting fashion, as if it were an exercise in total recall. I cannot even remember poems I *myself* wrote and wouldn't attempt reciting them without the printed words in front of me.

The poet Eve Merriam has stated, "I want children to love poetry, not memorize it."

I think all poets feel the same way, and I hope that one day all adults will too.

Unfortunately, too many children with unpleasant experiences with poetry have grown up to become teachers of children. I find from working with young teachers that many fears exist. Lee Shapiro, a first-year student teacher in my graduate course in Children's Literature and Story Telling at the City College of New York, wrote me:

The children I work with are 2½ and 3 years old plus. I feel very unsure of what poems I should select for them, which will be appropriate within their capabilities of understanding.

I have felt for a long time that the structured introduction of poetry which I received in public and high school was frustrating and restricting besides being very painful. Being forced to analyze and dissect poetry did not leave me much room for enjoyment. Until very recently I have avoided any kind of poetry. Now I have begun to explore on my own with great satisfaction the world of poetry. How much I have missed!

As a young teenager I wanted adventure, mystery, murder, passion. It wasn't until my adult years that I realized that Shakespeare and poets like Noyes could have given me what I wanted then. Certainly the tragedies of Shakespeare dealt more passionately and romantically with life than did the drugstore magazines I bought with my weekly allowance. But I wasn't aware of this because I had to concentrate on analyzing meaningless phrases.

9

The 1970's were ushered in with a flood of tears by many teenagers via Erich Segal's popular novel and film *Love Story.* Most teens thought that Oliver and Jennifer, the hero and heroine, had *discovered* love just as most pre-schoolers think *Sesame Street* invented the alphabet!

I discussed *Love Story* and its characters with one group of students and helped them discover other love affairs in literature. Shakespeare's *Romeo and Juliet* took on a new meaning; it was suddenly all relevant. A reading of Elizabeth Barrett Browning's "How Do I Love Thee?" produced many wet eyes from the boys in the class as well as the girls. Tying in today with yesterday is a good way to introduce poetry. Handed coldly to these same students, "How Do I Love Thee?" would have brought guffaws, but relating it to Oliver and Jennifer made it all seem quite real, quite now.

"Children just don't enjoy poetry!"—or so I've been told over and over again. Perhaps we should stop and analyze why so many children do not like poetry. Firstly, in many cases poetry is *assigned* to be read. "Read the poem on page 16 and write your reactions to it" is a task I've heard given to children. Poetry isn't meant to be read and written about. Poetry is meant to be heard—said, sung, shouted, heard exuberantly!

There is no trickery involved in reading poems aloud. Often I'm asked, "How do you read a poem aloud to children?" The answer is simply, "Read a poem you like aloud to children." When a poem is read aloud with sincerity, boys and girls will enjoy its rhythm and its music and will understand its meaning without having to write about it.

I have found that the five guidelines below can help those who get butterflies in their stomachs when it comes to presenting poetry. These same points can be shared with children for they, too, should be reading and sharing poetry aloud:

1. Before reading a poem to the class, read it aloud several times by yourself to get the feel of the words and rhythm. Know the poem well. Mark the words and phrases you'd like to emphasize, and then you'll read it exactly as you feel it.

2. Follow the rhythm of the poem, reading it naturally. The physical appearance of most poems on the printed page dictate the rhythm and the mood of the words. Some poems are meant to be read softly and slowly; others must be read at a more rapid pace.

3. Make pauses that please you—pauses that make sense. Some poems sound better when the lines are rhythmically strung together. Sometimes great effects can be obtained by pausing at the end of each line. Many of the poems by e. e. cummings and William Carlos Williams convey greater mood when they are read by pausing at the end of each short line, as though you were saying something yourself for the first time, thinking of a word or words that will come from your tongue next. Isn't this how we speak? We think as we talk. Sometimes words flow easily—

> other times—
> they
> come
> slowly,
> thinking-ly,
> from our
> mouths.

4. When reading poems aloud, speak in a natural voice. Don't change to a high-pitched or bass-pitched tone. Read a poem as though you are telling your class about a new car or a television program you saw last night. Again, you must

be sincere. A poem must interest you as well as being one that you feel is right for your students.

5. After a poem is read, be quiet. Don't feel trapped into asking children questions such as, "Did you like that?" Most of the class will answer, "Yes!"—even if they didn't like it because *you* read it. And what if they didn't like it? By the time you begin finding out the reasons, the poem is destroyed and half of the class will see why they, too, shouldn't like it anymore!

A second reason children may find poetry distasteful is that it is often taught or presented via a unit approach. There are many places within the school day where a poem fits snugly. For instance, you can precede a mathematics lesson with Carl Sandburg's delightful "Arithmetic"; or a space poem might tie in with current events, or a poem can simply bring a little laughter into the day. The unit approach is good for social studies, mathematics, and science—but not for poetry!

A frequent mistake is making children memorize certain poems and/or asking them countless questions about the meanings of words and phrases. Unfortunately, there is available a steady stream of curriculum guides which suggest dissecting poems to the point of the ridiculous. I'll cite one example. In one guide the poem "City" by Langston Hughes is reprinted. The poem, a mere eight lines, beautifully describes a city waking up and going to bed. The guide suggests that after reading the poem aloud to children: "Ask: What is a city? Name some cities. How does a city spread its wings? What does the poet mean when he says 'making a song in stone that sings?' How can a city go to bed? How can a city hang lights? Where would a city's head be?"

The guide then suggests that children memorize the poem as a group lesson by rote:

The teacher will tell the children, "I'm going to say the first two lines. Then you will say them with me. Are you listening?" Get the attention of all. Say the first two lines.

Then the teacher says the next two lines. Then teacher and pupils repeat. Then teacher says the four lines of the first stanza. Then teacher and pupils say the four lines together.

Then the teacher mouths the first four lines as the children say them aloud reading teacher's lips. Teacher may assist with a word or two if the children falter.

Then have the children say the first four lines with appropriate gestures.

Review the poem everyday as the class gets clothing or is sitting quietly waiting for the bell to ring. This poem can then be used for assembly programs or entertainment when aboard a bus on trips or in a unit culmination.

To summarize, ask the children: "What did we learn from our lessons?"

After this nonsensical interrogation (billed in the guide as an "appreciation lesson") it would take a miracle or a child masochist to ever ask for this—or any other—poem again.

Probably one of the saddest commentaries on the compulsion to analyze in the history of poetry are the endless definitions and interpretations of Robert Frost's famous four-stanza, sixteen-line poem "Stopping by Woods on a Snowy Evening." Even poet-critics themselves are guilty of endless analysis. John Ciardi, in an article "Robert Frost: The Way to the Poem" (*Saturday Review,* April 12, 1958), takes more than seventy long lines to "explain" the hidden meanings.

In his book *The Pursuit of Poetry* (Simon & Schuster, 1969, p. 83) Louis Untermeyer, noted critic and anthologist, elaborates on this tearing apart of Frost's poem and includes the poet's own wry reaction to all this:

"I've been more bothered with that one than anybody has ever been with any poem in just pressing it with more than it should be pressed for. It means enough without being pressed." Disturbed by "pressers" puzzling about the snowy woods and the miles to go, he said that all the poem means is: "It's all very nice here, but I must be getting home. There are chores to do." At another time when a critic indicated that the last three lines implied that the poet longed for an after-life in heaven, Frost smiled and shook his head. "No, it only means I want to get the hell out of there."

Children, too, "want to get the hell out of there!"

Long before he enters school, long before he can read a printed word, the young child can be heard chanting familiar Mother Goose rhymes—verses that have come down through centuries. The young child voluntarily reciting Mother Goose melodies doesn't stop to ponder over the meanings of words unfamiliar to him. He doesn't know, and may never know what *curds* or *whey* are; nor does he know or care about the hidden personages behind peculiar names such as Wee Willie Winkle, Little Bo Beep, or the Queen of Hearts. To acquaint very young children with the fact that Mother Goose rhymes were political lampoons or satires about such historical figures as Mary Tudor, Henry VIII, or Mary, Queen of Scots would be ludicrous. None of this matters. The child is in love with the easy rhymes, the alliteration, the quick action, and the humor that Mother Goose contains.

Here, then, is the beginning of a love of poetry. If only we could preserve and nurture this love of rhyme and rhythm and the feeling for words that the young child has in him. He hears jingles on television daily; the radio and phonograph blare tunes that either parents, peers, or older siblings play incessantly. Like the Mother Goose rhymes, a four-year-old can sing lyrics to a popular song without *ever* seeing the words in print. He learns the words by repetition and love of a particular word scheme. And check out the average ten-, eleven- or twelve-year-old or teenager and see how many pop-rock rhythms he knows! Young people are entranced, almost mesmerized by their personal poets—the Beatles, Simon and Garfunkel, Bob Dylan—who all cry of love, sex, and the inequities of life. These children don't stop and ask each other what hidden meaning lies behind "Bridge Over Troubled Water" or "Let It Be."

In an interview with me the poet Myra Cohn Livingston agrees with this assessment (*Books Are by People,* Citation Press 1969, p. 153):

> ... the young people are listening, imaginatively involved with the symbolism that is much the same symbolism that man has always used, the rain, wind, sun and fantasy-escape symbolism—yellow submarines, tangerine trees, marshmallow skies. They are responding to the *total involvement,* which is at the basis of poetry, with the head, mind, heart, and body.

What is poetry? Perhaps the question is best posed in Eleanor Farjeon's poem "Poetry":

> What is Poetry? Who knows?
> Not a rose, but the scent of the rose;
> Not the sky, but the light in the sky;
> Not the fly, but the gleam of the fly;
> Not the sea, but the sound of the sea;
> Not myself, but what makes me
> See, hear, and feel something that prose
> Cannot: and what it is, who knows?

We really don't know what poetry is, but we do know what it should do, what it should evoke in each and every one of us. Through poetry we *should* "see, hear, and feel something that prose cannot."

What is poetry? When you find it, when you come across the something that says, "I can see it! I can hear it! I can feel it!"—and when you know that neither you nor your children may never seem the same again, you'll have found out what poetry truly is.

FOR FURTHER READING

Arbuthnot, May Hill, and Gina Sutherland. *Children and Books,* 4th ed. Chicago: Scott-Foresman, 1972.

Part two contains information on Mother Goose and ballads; part three, "Sing It Again," has three chapters on poetry past and present.

Arnstein, Flora J. *Poetry and the Young Child* (originally titled *Poetry in the Elementary Classroom*). New York: Dover Publications, 1971, pap.

How do you interest children in poetry? How do you get them to write it? What can a teacher do when required to teach poetry when he feels his background in the subject is inadequate? These questions are expertly answered in this publication prepared by the National Council of Teachers of English and first published by Appleton-Century-Crofts in 1962.

Clare, Sister Francis. "Poetry and Teach-Ins an 'In Thing'," *Elementary English,* April 1972, pp. 625–628.

Sister Francis, a teacher at Loyola High School in Monkato, Minnesota, describes an exciting, innovative approach to poetry with a group of 115 freshmen in five ninth-grade English classes Many ideas are shared that can easily be adapted for upper elementary grades. The article best sums up Sister Francis' approach by a statement from one of the participating students who states: "As for me, it deepened my interest and respect for which I considered before the drab old world of poetry . . ."

16

Conrad, Lawrence H. "Stimulate, Don't Mutilate," *NJEA Review*, September, 1966, pp. 28–9.

Dr. Conrad makes a plea to teachers to avoid the many pitfalls of ruining poetry for children. A good discussion with great insight into children's feelings.

Georgiou, Constantine. *Children and Their Literature*. Englewood Cliffs, N.J.: Prentice-Hall, 1969.

In chapter five the author includes an annotated listing of "Books of Poetry and Verse," which is worth looking at.

Haviland, Virginia, and William Jay Smith, comps. *Children and Poetry: A Selected, Annotated Bibliography*. Washington, D.C.: Government Printing Office, 1969.

A handsome, inexpensive (75¢) paperback bibliography, published in connection with the celebration of the fiftieth anniversary of National Children's Book Week. The annotations are lengthy; the list a bit too selective.

Huck, Charlotte S., and Doris Young Kuhn. *Children's Literature in the Elementary School,* 2nd ed. New York: Holt, Rinehart and Winston, 1968.

In chapter eight the authors define poetry for today's children and discuss selecting and sharing poetry. Many poems illustrate the author's views.

Larrick, Nancy. *A Parent's Guide to Children's Reading,* 3rd ed. New York: Doubleday, 1969; also available in paperback from Pocket Books.

See chapter ten, "Poetry for Everyone," wherein Dr. Larrick gives a general guide to poetry through topics such as "Find the Time—Choose the Place," "Selecting Poems to Read Aloud" and "Seeing Through the Poet's Eyes." On pages 240–249 there is a listing of collections of books by individual poets and anthologies of poetry.

Painter, Helen M. *Poetry and Children*. Newark, Dela.: International Reading Association, 1970.

A paperbound publication giving a general guide to using poetry in elementary classrooms. The bulk of the book, pages 20–83, "Suggestions for Guidance Into Poetry," gives many ideas and sums up a host of journal articles about poetry.

Raspanti, Sister Celeste. "He'll Sing Too Far—Some Thoughts on Teaching Poetry." *Elementary English,* March 1970, pp. 403–7.
A fine article discussing the realm of poetry and how it came, and should come—from the mouth of the poet to the ears of his listeners—until we learn the poems by heart, willingly.

Read, Herbert, comp. *This Way, Delight.* New York: Pantheon, 1956.
Sir Herbert discusses "What is Poetry?" on pages 137–43, in this anthology for children in the middle grades.

Trefethen, Florence. *Writing A Poem.* Boston: The Writer, 1970.
This text is for the adult and is designed to help the beginner or the experienced poet shape his poetic ideas into finished poems. It gives the reader great insight into the making of a poem and discusses both traditional and experimental verse forms. Many poems by well-known poets are given within the text as examples.

Untermeyer, Louis. *The Pursuit of Poetry.* New York: Simon and Schuster, 1969.
An interesting text for adult readers divided into two parts. Part one examines poetry, giving the reader a realization of the sense and essence of the poetic art. Part two is a handbook—an invaluable aid to teachers on any grade level—containing a compact and conversational encyclopedia of poetic terms, including examples of every pattern and form.

Wickens, Elaine. "Please Don't Tell the Children." *Young Children,* October 1967, pp. 15–18.
The author discusses the creativity developed by looking at and listening to a child's response to a poem.

Witucke, Virginia. *Poetry in the Elementary School.* Dubuque, Iowa: William C. Brown, 1970.

A good paperbound handbook citing many ideas and materials for presenting poetry in the elementary grades.

From *Animal Parade*, illustrated by Virginia Parsons. Copyright © 1970 by Doubleday and Company, Inc. Reproduced by permission of the publisher.

FROM MOTHER GOOSE
TO DR. SEUSS

POETS FOR PRIMARY AND
MIDDLE-GRADE STUDENTS

Maybe it was Mother Goose who began poetry for children when she took *muffett* and rhymed it with *tuffet,* played around with thumb and plum, and thought up "Hi diddle diddle/The cat and the fiddle."

There are many explanations of who the real Mother Goose was. Scholars differ: some claim she was the Queen of Sheba; others say her origin is French, or British, or German. Some say the name is *just* a name that originated in Boston. Others assert that the moniker was coined by Thomas Fleet, a well-known Boston printer whose mother-in-law's name was Elizabeth Vergoose. It is said that Fleet printed the very first collection of Mother Goose verses in 1719. Whoever Mother Goose was and wherever the rhymes really originated, they are still an integral ingredient of early childhood and world literature.

Why has Mother Goose had such wide appeal to generation after generation of young children? If we stop to look and listen to the rhymes, we can see that they awaken a responsiveness in children for they are short, fun-filled, dramatic, pleasing to the ear, easy to remember—and hard to forget.

The step from Mother Goose to other forms of poetry is a small one. Many boys and girls today quickly go from Mother Goose to the nonsense rhymes of Dr. Seuss—a man whose language and characters enchant them. We may never know the true origin of Mother Goose, but we do know that Dr. Seuss is an American and that he is alive and well and living in California. The Doctor, whose real name is Theodor Seuss Geisel, was born in Springfield, Massachusetts, in 1904. His first book, *And to Think That I Saw It on Mulberry Street* (Vanguard Press, 1937), was immediately acclaimed. Seussian characters thereafter have captured the minds and hearts of youngsters. Many educators argue whether or not Dr. Seuss' later works, such as *The Cat in the Hat* (Random House, 1957) and *The Cat in the Hat Comes Back* (Random House, 1958) are really good rhymes. Well, this all depends on one's definition of good rhyme. Is Mother Goose good rhyme? Does it really matter?

Mother Goose has been around for centuries, and I am sure the Seuss rhymes will be too. His unforgettable characters— the grinches and sneetches and drum-tummied snumms—will probably match Mother Goose's classic characters—pie-men and pumpkin eaters and pretty maids all in a row.

If children love Dr. Seuss, why not give his poetry to them? In 1968, the R. R. Bowker Company of New York published a list of the top fifteen best sellers in the children's book field from 1895–1965. Numbers nine and fourteen on the list, *The Cat in the Hat* and *The Cat in the Hat Comes Back,* showed total sales of 1,588,972 and 1,148,669 copies respectively— figures that attest to children's love of this funny rhymist.

In an interview I conducted with Dr. Seuss I asked him, "What is rhyme?" "Rhyme?" he answered, "A rhyme is something without which I would probably be in the dry cleaning business!" The dry cleaning business lost a great man, but the world gained from his clever pen. Thank goodness!

Children are raised on Dr. Seuss rhymes. Unfortunately that is where many stop, because that is where adults often leave them. With careful guidance children can learn to love poetry written by other contemporary poets, many of whom will be discussed within this chapter.

My own four-year-old niece can recite Mother Goose and Dr. Seuss rhymes the way a fourth-grader can recite his multiplication tables. On a recent visit to her house, I discussed several of the books in her library.

"What books are your best, best books?" I asked.

Without hesitation she gathered a stack from her shelf. Included in the selection were *Brian Wildsmith's Mother Goose* (Franklin Watts, 1963), Ezra Jack Keats' *The Snowy Day* (Viking, 1962), Margaret Wise Brown's *Where Have You Been?* (Scholastic Book Services), several titles by Dr. Seuss, and *The Secret Place and Other Poems* by Dorothy Aldis (Scholastic Book Services). All the volumes were books of verse except, of course, Keats' *The Snowy Day*.

"Why is this one of your best best?" I asked, pointing to *The Snowy Day*.

"I like Peter and I like the words *crunch, crunch, crunch* and *plop*," Kim giggled.

"Why do you like this one?" I asked, picking up *Mother Goose*.

"Because it's funny," she chuckled.

"And this?" pointing to the Dorothy Aldis collection.

"'Cause this book's about me!" she replied.

What perceptive comments. What sheer delight. Kim, at four, had taken the small step and progressed from Mother Goose to Dr. Seuss to Dorothy Aldis. And this is poetry that she will enjoy and come back to time and time again throughout her childhood years.

If only all children could be fed on this feast of literature. If only adult critics would stop shoving down their throats things that children aren't ready for—only to make them dislike poetry.

ROBERT LOUIS STEVENSON—PROS AND CONS

In her article "Young Children Enjoy Poetry" (*Elementary English,* January 1966, pp. 56–9), Grace Pitman, a third-grade teacher in West Lafayette, Indiana, reports on a study she conducted with sixteen boys and sixteen girls who came from a high socio-economic level. Miss Pitman selected fifty poems from recommended anthologies of poetry for children for her study—poems varied in interest and subject matter and included works from traditional Mother Goose to contemporary John Ciardi. It was "discovered" that children enjoyed poems relating to their own experiences.

It is interesting to note that poems by Robert Louis Stevenson appeared among the ten most enjoyed poems and the ten most disliked poems. Too often we educators stick to the familiar and rely too heavily on the works of Stevenson throughout the primary grades. *A Child's Garden of Verses,* in one form or another, seems to be one of the poetic Bibles in elementary classrooms and school and public libraries.

Too often Stevenson's work is read and re-read without stopping to find out if girls and boys truly enjoy it. I am sure that if all of Stevenson's works were forced upon Kim rather than the variety of books she has been given, she'd quickly set aside poetry. There is much of Robert Louis Stevenson that still works well today, but the best of it has found its way into anthologies where it should be. Too much Stevenson too soon can quickly deter children from taking that important step. Young children need Mother Goose and Dr. Seuss; they need the funny; they need good literature with words that please their ears like the *crunch* and *plop* that Peter experienced in *The Snowy Day.* They need poems where they can see themselves being alone, dropping a jelly sandwich, or looking at a lion in the zoo. Girls and boys need to look at, see, and feel the *me* in poetry.

In Miss Pitman's class, Stevenson's "The Land of Story-books" ranked number ten of the ten most enjoyed poems:

> At evening when the lamp is lit,
>   Around the fire my parents sit;
>   They sit at home and talk and sing,
>   And do not play at anything.
>
> Now, with my little gun, I crawl
>   All in the dark along the wall,
>   And follow round the forest track
>   Away behind the sofa back.
>
> There, in the night, where none can spy,
>   All in my hunter's camp I lie,
>   And play at books that I have read
>   Till it is time to go to bed.
>
> These are the hills, these are the woods,
>   These are my starry solitudes;
>   And there the river by whose brink
>   The roaring lions come to drink.
>
> I see the others far away
>   As if in firelit camp they lay,
>   And I, like to an Indian scout,
>   Around their party prowled about.
>
> So, when my nurse comes in for me,
>   Home I return across the sea,
>   And go to bed with backward looks
>   At my dear land of Story-books.

There is a good bit of fantasy within this poem and, more important, the *me* comes through. When I have used this poem in classrooms, one child always wants to know if the child in the poem is sick. Most children today think that a nurse is synonymous with illness.

Stevenson's "Autumn Fires" ranked number nine among the ten most disliked poems:

> In the other gardens
>   And all up the vale,
> From the autumn bonfires
>   See the smoke trail!
>
> Pleasant summer over
>   And all the summer flowers,
> The red fire blazes,
>   The gray smoke towers.
>
> Sing a song of seasons!
>   Something bright in all!
> Flowers in the summer,
>   Fires in the fall!

There is certainly little of "me," fantasy, or adventure within these three stanzas. Miss Pitman's third-graders were quite sharp in their choices. Perhaps the autumn fires that Mr. Stevenson wrote about in the late 1800's are somewhat burned out now.

Giving children a feast of poetry in their early childhood years nurtures a love of poetry. As children grow, mature, and develop new interests and new tastes, they can be led to poems that express broader visions of the world. Today publishers are offering a growing number of excellent books of poetry for boys and girls. Volumes of original verse and specialized and generalized anthologies appear on publishers' lists each season. Since it is difficult for teachers to keep abreast of what poetry is available for children, the remainder of this chapter will explore poetry for the young child and for children in the middle grades through a discussion of poets and their work.

POETS FOR THE YOUNG CHILD

As teachers you will want to become acquainted with some of the more popular contemporary poets who write specifically for young children. Mention cannot be made of all the many poets who have contributed to this area of children's literature, but the following is a sampling of one dozen American poets who have written several volumes of original verse and whose works have been widely anthologized. This information can also serve to introduce some of the best poetry to boys and girls for they may be motivated to read the poetry after you have fed them personal anecdotes about the writers' lives and their work.

In Appendix I, "Poetry in Paperback: A Selected Listing," I have included anthologies containing works of both the new and the older master poets such as Robert Louis Stevenson, A. A. Milne, Walter de la Mare, and others on whom we have all been brought up. It is neither my contention nor intention to throw away all that is old; but a desire to bring the new and the now into the lives of children leads me to emphasize here contemporary poets.

DOROTHY ALDIS

Dorothy Aldis was born in Chicago in 1897. She raised four children, had several grandchildren, and always found time to write. She published over twenty-seven books; her stories and poems can be found in hundreds of schoolbooks and anthologies. The poet died in 1966.

Mrs. Aldis' poems truly touch upon the everyday experiences of childhood. Throughout a child's early years he is concerned with himself—the things *he* does, what appeals to *him* most. Aldis saw this through a poet's eye and wrote of the simple daily routines in which children participate. She wrote of a child's interest in himself in poems such as "My Nose," "Going to Sleep," and "See, I Can Do It,"—a delightful, different look at a child brushing his teeth. She wrote of a child's emotions in "Alone," which is about a child left out of play because he didn't know the group of youngsters. In the poem "The Secret Place," the poet describes a tree where a child can escape with his own thoughts.

I have never seen a child totally reject the poems of Dorothy Aldis. Yet, in a recent roundup review of several contemporary volumes of poetry, Selden Rodman, an anthologist who collects poems for adult audiences, dismisses the work of Aldis as being banal and states that a recent collection, *Favorite Poems of Dorothy Aldis* (Putnam, 1970), "sounds like a put on and reads like one."

One wonders if critics such as this know very much about the young child and his early interests. Mr. Rodman is entitled to his opinion—but look at the work of Aldis and judge for yourself. I think you'll enjoy meeting her.

Poems from Mrs. Aldis' first four books have been collected into one volume, *All Together* (Putnam, 1952). This collection contains 144 poems just right for the pre-school and primary-aged child. Four other books of hers are *Hello Day* (Putnam, 1959), *Quick as a Wink* (Putnam, 1960), a picture book paperback collection containing thirty poems, *The Secret Place and Other Poems* (Scholastic Book Services), delightfully illustrated by Olivia H. H. Cole, and *Is Anybody Hungry?* (Putnam, 1964), which describes the eating habits of animals, insects, youngsters, and even flowers who get a "lovely long drink" now and then.

GWENDOLYN BROOKS

Gwendolyn Brooks is the first black woman to win the Pulitzer Prize for Poetry. She received this award in 1950 for a volume of her adult poems, *Annie Allen* (Harper and Row, 1949). Most of the poet's work is directed to mature students and adults. Miss Brooks was born in Topeka, Kansas, on June 7, 1917. At an early age she moved to Chicago, where she still resides. Recently she was named Poet Laureate of the State of Illinois, succeeding the late Carl Sandburg. She is married to Henry Blakely and is the mother of two children.

Through her poetry, Miss Brooks speaks of life's harsh realities; her words are vivid and compassionate and speak about the black experience.

Unfortunately, the poet has only written one volume of poems for younger boys and girls, *Bronzeville Boys and Girls* (Harper and Row, 1956). It contains poignant views of children living in the crowded conditions of an American inner-city. Each of the thirty-four poems bears the name of an individual child and is devoted to his thoughts, feelings, and emotions. There is "Val" who does not like the sound "when grown-ups at parties are laughing," and who would "rather be in the basement," or "rather be outside"; "Keziah" who has a secret place to go; "Paulette" who questions her mother's advice about growing up, posing "What good is sun/If I can't run?," and "Robert, Who Is Often a Stranger to Himself."

When I compiled *Me! A Book of Poems* (Seabury, 1970), I included Miss Brooks' "Skipper" from *Bronzeville Boys and Girls*—a poem about the death of a pet goldfish. In a guide to the book I commented that I well remembered as a child the day one of my pet goldfish died. I wasn't terribly upset by its death but was rather taken aback by an aunt's advice to "Flush it down the toilet." I listened to her. I did what she said. But wouldn't the experience have been richer for me if, instead, I had been given a poem such as "Skipper"? Perhaps I too, like the child in the poem, would have buried my fish beneath a tree. And perhaps I would have come to understand much sooner the value of poetry.

Bronzeville Boys and Girls is one book that should be in every school library, available when you want and need it. And you will—time and time again.

BEATRICE SCHENK DE REGNIERS

Beatrice Schenk de Regniers' book *Something Special* (Harcourt, 1958) is just that! Here are ten rhymes that will delight young children. "What Did You Put in Your Pocket?" is a chant; "If We Walked on Our Hands" is gay nonsense about a "mixed up/fixed up/topsy turvey/sit-u-a-tion"; "Little Sounds" gives insight into how wonderful our sense of hearing can be. The volume is illustrated by Irene Haas.

Mrs. de Regniers was born in Lafayette, Indiana; she now lives in New York City with her husband, Francis. She has written more than twenty books—most of which have a poetic touch including *May I Bring A Friend?* (Atheneum, 1964), winner of the 1965 Caldecott Medal, *A Little House of Your Own* (Harcourt, 1954), *A Boy, A Rat and a Butterfly* (Atheneum, (1971) in which Peter, the Rat, recites the poetry of Keats and Shelley, and *Red Riding Hood* (Atheneum, 1972), the classic fairytale retold in verse.

Currently Mrs. de Regniers is the editor of Scholastic Book Services' Lucky Book Club.

AILEEN FISHER

Aileen Fisher weaves together the world of childhood and the world of nature in her poetry. One of her *musts* for the elementary classroom is the recently published *In One Door and Out the Other* (T. Y. Crowell, 1970). More than half the verses in this book are new; others were published in earlier collections including her first book, *The Coffee-Pot Face* (McBride and Company; out of print), published in 1933. In this book she describes the mischievous joys and inevitable frustrations of early childhood. There are verses about "Peeking" at father sleeping, "Growing," and "A Birthday"—"the next best thing to Christmas." The text is illustrated by Lillian Hoban. Miss Fisher has also written longer, narrative poems dealing with nature. These include *Listen, Rabbit* (T. Y. Crowell, 1964) and *Sing Little Mouse* (T. Y. Crowell, 1969), both lavishly illustrated by Symeon Shimin; a delightful tale, *Clean as a Whistle* (T. Y. Crowell, 1969), about three grimy children who are loath to leave the woods to face a bathtub; an interesting volume, *But Ostriches...* (T. Y. Crowell, 1970), in which Miss Fisher muses in verse about ostriches, who are among the most curious creations in nature, and their peculiarities, and *Feathered Ones and Furry* (T. Y. Crowell, 1971), verses about birds and animals.

A trip to the library will enable you to peruse other books by this poet. Miss Fisher has also written plays and programs, prose about nature and American heritage, biographies, Bible themes, and articles for leading magazines and journals.

Miss Fisher currently lives in Boulder, Colorado. Regarding poetry, her first love, she told me: "Poetry is a rhythmical piece of writing that leaves the reader feeling that life is a little richer than before, a little more full of wonder, beauty, or just plain delight."

Miss Fisher can be heard reading thirty-one of her poems on the recording *Poetry Parade,* available from Weston Woods. The recording also contains readings by Harry Behn, David McCord, and Karla Kuskin.

KATHLEEN FRASER

Kathleen Fraser's first book of poetry for children appeared in 1968, a cleverly executed volume titled *Stilts, Somersaults, and Headstands* (Atheneum). The poems are game poems based on the painting "Children's Games" by Peter Breughel the Elder.

The idea came to her while traveling through Europe with her husband, Jack Marshall, the poet and novelist. When she saw the Breughel painting, she was struck by how many of the 400-year-old games had figured prominently in her own childhood. Thus, we have poems about hoops and hobbyhorses, blowing bubbles, and blindman's bluff.

The text is a delight to share with children and can be used in a variety of ways. Mrs. Fraser's poems for adults have appeared in leading journals, including *Mademoiselle* for which she was once an assistant editor.

MARGARET HILLERT

Margaret Hillert has been a first-grade teacher in Royal Oak Park, Michigan, for over twenty years. Her poetry, first published several years ago, has appeared in children's magazines such as *Humpty Dumpty's Magazine* and *Jack and Jill.*

In 1969 Follett published *Farther Than Far.* Most of the poems had previously appeared in a variety of magazines and newspapers including *The Instructor* and *The Christian Science Monitor*. The poems in this slim volume will have special appeal to pre-schoolers and primary-aged girls and boys. The verses deal with everything the young child is interested in from the ABC's to "space and space and space."

In a letter Miss Hillert shared with me her philosophy of poetry:

> I can't give you a glib one-line definition of poetry such as many I have seen. Poetry has been an undefined but definite part of my life, and I don't think I chose to write it at all. I have been writing it ever since the first one I did when I was eight years old, which seems to indicate it has always been a part of my nature. I read widely, from the poetry stacks in the library when I was growing up—and still do to some extent. I'm not one of those people who can say, "Today I'll write a poem." I may go without writing anything for some time as a consequence, but once I get the grain of an idea, the thing must be worked through, sometimes for days, weeks, or months. Things don't usually come to me whole and full blown. It intrigues me to work generally, but not always, with traditional forms but in fresh ways.
>
> For me, poetry is great fun and consists mostly in reading lots of it—both to myself and to the first graders I teach.

PATRICIA HUBBELL

Patricia Hubbell was born in Bridgeport, Connecticut. She has written three volumes of poetry for children: *The Apple Vendor's Fair* (1963), *8 A.M. Shadows* (1965), and *Catch Me a Wind* (1968; all published by Atheneum.) The poet's range of interests is quite varied. In *8 A.M. Shadows* you'll find poems about "Squirrels" and "Bedtime"; in *The Apple Vendor's Fair* are poems about animals and a toll-taker. One poem in this book that appeals to listeners of all ages is "When Dinosaurs Ruled the Earth"—a rhythmical poem telling about the brontosaurus, diplodocus, gentle trachodon, and what they did once-upon-a-time. *Catch Me a Wind* contains poems that will appeal to all age groups; poems that young audiences will especially enjoy are "Tree House," "Shadows," and "To a Giraffe." Older girls and boys will enjoy "Message from a Mouse Ascending from a Rocket" and a longer poem, "At Little League."

When the poet is not writing poetry she is busy writing a weekly column, "Kennel and Stable," for the *Bridgeport Sunday Post*. She is a lifelong horsewoman and mulls over many of her poems while riding her Appaloosa through the woods of Connecticut. Her husband is a newspaperman; they live in Easton, Connecticut, with their two children, several ponies, dogs, cats, and a goat.

KARLA KUSKIN

Whenever I think of the poetry of Karla Kuskin, I think of a teacher I met while conducting a week-long poetry workshop at the University of Nevada in Las Vegas. This teacher "found" Karla Kuskin and delighted in sharing her humorous poems with the class. Each day she would come into class smiling, with one of the poet's books in her hands. "Do you know Hughbert?" she'd ask. Without waiting for an answer she'd read aloud a poem, in this case "Hughbert and the Glue," which is typical of the very funny poems in Mrs. Kuskin's books. Hughbert is a child who gets a jar of glue and glues himself, his mother, brother, and his pets all to one another. The poem is contained in *The Rose on My Cake* (Harper and Row, 1964).

Mrs. Kuskin's books of verses are just right for young children—and for their teachers, too. Besides writing the poems, Mrs. Kuskin illustrates her own books with stylized pictures.

In *Alexander Soames: His Poems* (Harper and Row, 1962) Alexander's mother asks him for his thoughts on dancing, beetles, knitting, and various other subjects, and young Master Soames comments invariably come out of his mouth in rhyme. *Sand and Snow* (Harper and Row, 1965) contrasts two children's views of summer and winter. *The Rose on My Cake* and *In the Middle of the Trees* (Harper and Row, 1958) are collections of gay verse. Two favorites with children in the latter include "Lewis Had a Trumpet," about a boy in love with the instrument, and "Catherine," about a girl who bakes a most delicious mud, sticks, and stones cake.

The Rose on My Cake contains seventeen precious tidbits including "I Woke Up This Morning," a poem that is perfect for reading, even yelling, aloud. It is three pages long and tells of a young child who wakes up and can do nothing right (one of those days we all have). As the child's frustrations mount, so does the type in the book, becoming larger and larger, making the poem funnier and funnier.

Of course, there is a serious side to Mrs. Kuskin also. In tender poems she writes of a child "Within a Wood" and children digging in "Beaches" (both from *The Rose on My Cake*). Her latest book *Any Me I Want to Be* (Harper and Row, 1972), contains thirty poems.

Mrs. Kuskin has written several other poetry picture books too. She is married to an oboist, has a son and daughter, and lives in the Brooklyn Heights section of New York. She can be heard reading twenty-four of her poems on the recording *Poetry Parade,* available from Weston Woods. The recording also includes readings by David McCord, Harry Behn, and Aileen Fisher.

MYRA COHN LIVINGSTON

Myra Cohn Livingston is another poet who understands childhood experiences. A collection of her books rivals a good course in child development and/or child psychology. Her poems reflect the many moments and moods of growing up; they are filled with laughter, gaiety, curiosity, tenderness, sadness, and exuberance. Whether she is telling of whispers that "tickle through your ear," from her first book of poems, *Whispers and Other Poems* (Harcourt, 1958), or the story of Uncle Tiger, a cat who instinctively kills a scolding old blue-jay in "It Happens Once in Awhile" from *A Crazy Flight and Other Poems* (Harcourt, 1969), her use of words, rhythms, and various poetic forms evoke sharp moods and vivid mind-pictures.

Mrs. Livingston began writing poetry while a freshman at Sarah Lawrence College. She has recalled for my book *Books Are by People* (Citation Press, 1969, pp. 153–4):

I turned in some poems ("Whispers" and "Sliding among them) that my professor felt were for children. She urged me to submit them to *Story Parade* magazine; some were accepted. In 1946 "Whispers" became my first published poem. I submitted a complete manuscript, *Whispers and Other Poems,* to several publishing houses; it was rejected. Margaret McElderry of Harcourt urged me, however, to continue writing. Twelve years later I sent the manuscript back to her at Harcourt; it was accepted and published in 1958.

The poet is married to Richard Livingston, a CPA who has also published a children's book, *The Hunkendunkens* (Harcourt, 1968). The Livingstons have three children and live in Beverly Hills, California in an Italian villa built on three levels in the Santa Monica Mountains.

Mrs. Livingston was born on August 17, 1926, in Omaha, Nebraska, and told me (p. 155):

I had an ideal, happy childhood. I had wise and wonderful parents who taught me that a busy creative life brings much happiness. Today, I am a woman with a very full life. I have family, friends, a home I enjoy, a career that enables me to stay home most of the time, the opportunity to live in an exciting community, teach writing, share poetry with children, share my ideas with teachers and librarians, collect books, do bookbinding, and grow and pick flowers—and to keep the joys ahead of the troubles!

The poet's views and philosophy of poetry are expressed in other parts of this volume. Other books for younger readers (all published by Harcourt) by Mrs. Livingston include *Wide Awake* (1959), *I'm Hiding* (1961), *See What I Found* (1962), *I'm Not Me* (1963), *Happy Birthday* (1964), *The Moon and a Star* (1965), *I'm Waiting* (1966), *Old Mrs. Twindlytart* (1967); she has compiled two anthologies for older boys and girls, *A Tune Beyond Us* (1968) and *Speak Roughly to Your Little Boy: A Collection of Parodies and Burlesques, Together with the Original Poems* (1971), and two collections of original poems, *A Crazy Flight and Other Poems* (1969) and *Malibu and Other Poems,* her first book published by Atheneum (1972).

DAVID MC CORD

David McCord's subjects range from nature and the country to a trip to the laundromat, and he writes for both children and adults. In my interview with him he commented on this duality:

Poetry for children is simpler than poetry for adults. The overtones are fewer, but it should have overtones. Basically, of course, it isn't different. Children's verse sometimes turns out, or is turned out, to be not much more than doggerel: lame lines, limp rhymes, and poor ideas. By and large, verse written for children is rhymed; it is nearly always brief, though an occasional poem in the hands of a skilled performer like Ogden Nash may tell a story. But poetry, like rain, should fall with elemental music, and poetry for children should catch the eye as well as the ear and the mind. It should delight; it really *has* to delight. Furthermore, poetry for children should keep reminding them, without any feeling on their part that they are being reminded, that the English language is a most marvelous and availing instrument.

Mr. McCord's first book of poetry for children, *Far and Few* (Little, Brown, 1952; also available in paperback from Dell) tells about many simple nature images—a "Tiger Lily" who looks like a panther, "Father and I in the Woods," and "Fred," a flying squirrel. Other books include *Take Sky* (Little, Brown, 1962; also available in paperback from Dell) and *All Day Long* (Little, Brown, 1966). The whimsical *Every Time I Climb a Tree* (Little, Brown, 1967) is a selection of verses for young children from the three above collections; this picture book, illustrated by Caldecott Award winning artist Marc Simont, has sure-fire appeal to young children. Included are poems that are widely anthologized such as the title poem, "The Pickety Fence," and "This Is My Rock." These two poems plus twenty-one others are read by Mr. McCord on the recording *Poetry Parade,* available from Weston Woods. The recording also includes readings by Harry Behn, Karla Kuskin, and Aileen Fisher.

Mr. McCord was born on November 15, 1897, near New York's Greenwich Village. His ancestors were colonial Pennsylvanians. As a boy he lived on a ranch in the Rogue River Valley of Oregon, where he learned how to live in the wilderness. He is a graduate of Harvard, which recently conferred on him its first degree of Doctor of Humane Letters. He thinks that learning "The Owl and the Pussycat" by heart at five, the Morse Code at seven (he holds a very early government wireless operator's license), and commencing the study of Latin at ten began his lifelong interest in rhythm.

EVE MERRIAM

Eve Merriam is a poet who writes for all ages. Her recent adult books (both Simon and Schuster, 1969 and 1970) *Inner City Mother Goose* and *Nixon Poems* have been widely acclaimed. Most of her poetry for adults is concerned with her major life interests—social and political satire and the status of women in modern society.

The poet lives in New York City with her author-husband, Leonard C. Lewin; she has two children and a family cat, Towel. Miss Merriam has reminisced to me:

I was a born poet.... While in school I had my poetry published in various school publications. I wanted to get away from home; I wanted to meet other poets and to be in New York, the literary mecca.... I remembered reading somewhere that Carl Sandburg once worked in advertising, so I would, too. I got a job as an advertising copywriter on Madison Avenue and progressed to become a fashion editor for glamour magazines....

When my first poem was published in a poetry magazine, I could have been run over! ... It was in a little magazine printed on butcher paper, but it was gold to me.

For the young child Miss Merriam has a trilogy of books (all published by Atheneum): *Catch a Little Rhyme* (1966), *It Doesn't Always Have to Rhyme* (1964), and *There Is No Rhyme for Silver* (1962). Within this trilogy you'll find many poems to pick and choose from to use with youngsters. In *Catch a Little Rhyme,* Miss Merriam describes a building going up, "Bam, Bam, Bam;" what it is like to an animal

"Inside the Zoo;" and what would happen if the alphabet ran "Backwards."

"What in the World?" a delightful riddle poem about animals, can be found in *There Is No Rhyme for Silver,* along with "To Meet Mr. Lincoln."

Miss Merriam prepared brochures on each of the books in this trilogy; in one, "What Can a Poem Do?", she says:

A poem . . . is very much like you, and that is quite natural, since there is a rhythm in our own body; in your pulse, in your heart beat, in the way you breathe, laugh or cry; in the very way you speak . . . What can a poem do? Just about everything—even though there is no rhyme for silver.

> (Or orange.
> Any others?)

A recent volume, *Finding a Poem* (Atheneum, 1970), is particularly well suited to the middle-grade child. It includes an essay, "Writing A Poem," which traces the evolution of "Landscape," a two-stanza verse dealing with the environment. The essay makes interesting reading for the teacher as it explains how a poem is formed within the mind of this poet.

Miss Merriam can be heard reading several of her poems for children on the Caedmon recording, "To Catch a Little Rhyme," available from D. C. Heath and Company. This recording invites children to respond both verbally and with their whole bodies.

LILIAN MOORE

Lilian Moore's poems and stories have appeared in the popular *Humpty Dumpty's Magazine* since its inception. In 1967, Atheneum published her first book of poems, *I Feel the Same Way* (also available in paperback from Scholastic Book Services); two years later *I Thought I Heard the City* (Atheneum, 1969) appeared. Both volumes have a city feeling to them, although they can be read and shared with children everywhere. In *I Feel the Same Way,* the poet shares her secret poetic feelings; *I Thought I Heard the City* reveals images of foghorns in the bay, reflections through window-store panes, and pigeons who never sing. She commented to me:

I think I wrote most of the poems in *I Feel the Same Way* on my way to work. I think of them as my subway songs. Often when I seemed to be staring vacantly at subway ads, I was working intensely on a new idea. And sometimes when it didn't come off, I put it to bed at night, with a profound faith in my unconscious where the special truth I'm seeking usually begins.

Mrs. Moore was born in New York, attended public schools there, went to Hunter College, and did graduate work at Columbia University. She was a teacher and reading specialist and then worked for Scholastic Book Services for many years, pioneering the development of the company's Arrow Book Club, a paperback book club for children in grades four through six. Currently she lives in upstate New York on a farm with her husband; she has one teenage son.

POETS FOR THE MIDDLE-GRADE CHILD

Poetry for children in the middle grades should be introduced the same way it is to the younger set. If it is, children will come to know and love poetry and will continue the affection for it developed in younger years. Children in the upper grades should have poetry read aloud to them for its sheer delight and pleasure. Memorizing lines and/or entire poems is not necessary—and it can help destroy a love of poetry. Analyzing words and phrases are chores that should not be forced upon children. If children like a particular poem, they'll remember it, and even memorize it voluntarily.

In poetry, just as in any other subject, some children will like a particular selection and others will not. Some girls and boys like spinach and others detest it. And some children prefer swimming to skating. They should not feel they have to like a poem. Agreeing and disagreeing often makes the sharing of poetry an exciting part of the day.

It is wise to read a selection of your choice once to the class, then re-read it a second time. Eventually, children may ask you to read a particular poem again and again and again.

Below is a discussion of six popular contemporary poets who appeal to middle-grade girls and boys. Again, it must be emphasized that there is not enough space to mention all the poets who have contributed to this area of children's literature. This section will merely serve as an introduction to some of the best poetry you can bring into your classrooms so that your students can hear, read, and come to love the very best. Older students may be interested in the lives of these poets. Often getting to know something about a poet motivates children to read their works.

HARRY BEHN

In an article, "Poetry for Children" (*Horn Book,* April, 1966, pp. 163–75), Harry Behn commented:

The poems I shall write about must be mostly my own. They are all I know closely enough. Anything at too great a distance feathers away into a scholarly mist where I am lost and only my intellect can follow, and so all I can do is tell how I happened to write this poem or that—or any at all. I can only guess at what was derived from my own childhood and what I absorbed from my children and, more recently, from theirs.

Mr. Behn was fifty years old before he began writing for children. It all started one summer evening when his three-year-old daughter pointed to the stars and said, "Moon babies." The next day he wrote a poem for her and has been writing poetry ever since.

He was born in McCabe, Arizona, on September 24, 1898. He had the kind of childhood most children today would envy and can only live vicariously via television programs. He has written in a fact sheet distributed by Harcourt, Brace, Jovanovich's Children's Book Division:

When I was a small boy in Territorial Arizona, in the town of Prescott, in the Bradshaw Mountains, all the boys I played with were influenced by the Indians who lived in wickiups on their reservation across Granite Creek. Our parents could still remember massacres or narrow escapes from painted, yelping hostiles and did not love them.

The boys were not afraid of the Yavapais. We knew Apaches had been dangerous because they had been treated unfairly. But not even they had been as wicked as gamblers who shot each other once in a while in the bad part of town . . .

Upon graduating from high school he lived one summer with the Blackfeet tribe until his parents persuaded him to attend college. In 1922 he received a B.S. degree from Harvard University; the next year he went to Sweden as an American-Scandinavian Fellow. Following this he became involved in the arts and media, founding and editing *The Arizona Quarterly,* editing anthropological papers, writing movie scenarios, and teaching creative writing at the University of Arizona.

In 1947 he moved to Connecticut to write and travel. Mr. Behn has three children and several grandchildren.

His first book of poems for children, *The Little Hill* (Harcourt) appeared in 1949. The book contains thirty poems, many of which have been widely anthologized. Other books include *All Kinds of Time* (Harcourt, 1950), an unusual poetic picture book about clocks, time, and the seasons, and *Windy Morning* (Harcourt, 1953), a small volume containing many poems about nature and the seasons. Although the above titles are intended for girls and boys in the earlier grades, there are many poems applicable to all ages.

For children in the middle grades the poet has translated over eighty Japanese haiku in the volume *Cricket Songs* (Harcourt, 1964) with accompanying pictures chosen from the works of Japanese masters. Recently *More Cricket Songs* (Harcourt, 1971) was published following the same format as his earlier collection.

The Golden Hive (Harcourt, 1966) is a collection of Mr. Behn's own poems for older children, reflecting his joy in nature, his remembrance of his childhood, and his deep sense of the American past. Undoubtedly his concern for nature stems from his childhood years. In the fact sheet cited earlier, he wrote:

My earliest memory is of a profound and sunny peace, a change of seasons, spring to summer, summer to fall, and the wonder of being alive. Those are the mysteries I later tried to evoke in the poems I wrote about my childhood; the imprints of stillness determining which haiku I chose to translate . . .

Like all aborigines, children are accustomed to thinking about the beginnings of things, the creation of beauty, the wisdom of plants and animals, of how alive everything is, like stars and wildflowers, and how wonderfully different people can be from each other.

The poet has also written a book for adults expressing his views on poetry, *Chrysalis: Concerning Children and Poetry* (Harcourt, 1968). He can be heard reading his own poems on the recording *Poetry Parade,* available from Weston Woods. Although the recording is primarily for younger children, it can be used effectively with upper-grade students also. The recording also contains readings by Karla Kuskin, Aileen Fisher, and David McCord.

ROBERT FROST

Robert Lee Frost was born in San Francisco on March 26, 1874. He didn't attend school until he was about twelve years old and never read a book until he was fourteen. He has commented (Edward Connery Lathem, *Interviews with Robert Frost.* Holt, Rinehart and Winston, 1966, p. 90.): "...after I had my first book a new world opened up for me, and after that I devoured as many of them as I could lay my hands on. By the time I was 15, I was already beginning to write verses."

In 1885, after the death of his father, he moved with his mother and sister to Lawrence, Massachusetts, his father's birthplace. In 1890 his first poem, "La Noche Triste," was published in the school paper. In 1892 he graduated from Lawrence High School as co-valedictorian. The other student to win this honor was Eleanor White, who became his wife in 1895.

Frost attended Dartmouth College but left before taking term examinations to teach in his mother's private school. From 1897–1899 he attended Harvard University but left because of illness. He then bought a dairy farm in New Hampshire, but he failed as a farmer, went back to teaching, and constantly grew as a writer of poetry. In 1912, Frost, his wife, and four children moved to England. In 1913 his first book of poems was published, *A Boy's Will,* a collection of some thirty poems written between 1892–1912. The following year, *North of Baton* was published. Frost at age forty, had now earned a total of approximately $200 from his poetry.

In August of 1914, when war broke out, Frost moved his family back to the United States. When he arrived at Grand Central Station in New York City, he noticed on a newsstand the *New Republic* magazine with his name and the title, "Death of the Hired Man," on the cover. He soon learned that Henry Holt and Company was publishing his poetry in the United States; he remained with the company, now Holt, Rinehart and Winston, for his entire life.

During his lifetime honor upon honor was bestowed upon him. He was the only person ever to win four Pulitzer Prizes. His own life, however, was filled with personal tragedies. His sister, Jeanie, became mentally ill and was institutionalized; his daughter, Marjorie, died of childbirth, a year after her marriage; his only son, Carol, committed suicide; his daughter, Irma, was hospitalized as an invalid.

Frost's participation in the inauguration of President John F. Kennedy was a milestone in his career. People across the nation witnessed an unforgettable incident on this day, January 20, 1961. When the sun's glare and some gusty wind prevented the poet from reading "The Gift Outright," he put the sheet of paper in his overcoat pocket and recited it from memory.

On March 26, 1962, on his eighty-eighth birthday, Frost was awarded the Congressional Medal at the White House by President Kennedy. He died on January 23, 1963.

Boys and girls can read a short, easy-to-read biography of the poet in *Robert Frost: America's Poet* by Doris Faber (Prentice-Hall, 1964). An excellent book for teacher reference and for the mature reader is *Frost: The Poet and His Poetry* by David A. Sohn and Richard H. Tyre (Holt, 1967; also available in paperback from Bantam Books). In this volume the reader is given a concise introduction to the poet's life and works.

A book-record combination, *Frost Has a Say* is available from Holt also. Included with the book is a 7-inch LP recording on which the poet reads eight of his poems including "Birches" and "Stopping by Woods on a Snowy Evening." It will not be easy for youngsters to sit and listen to all of the selections at one sitting. If the record is used, it would be wise to play only one selection at a time rather than attempting to give them too much at one sitting.

Robert Frost's poems for children appear in *You Come Too* (Holt, 1959), a collection of fifty-one "favorite poems for young readers." Several recent anthologies contain poems by Frost: "Fireflies in the Garden" is included in *A Paper Zoo: A Collection Of Animal Poems by Modern American Poets* (Atheneum, 1968); six of his poems appear in *Piping Down the Valleys Wild* edited by Nancy Larrick (Delacorte, 1968; also available in paperback from Dell); "The Pasture" and "Stopping by Woods on a Snowy Evening" are in *The Arrow Book of Poetry* selected by Ann McGovern (Scholastic Book Services).

LANGSTON HUGHES

Langston Hughes was another of those multi-talented men who wrote and wrote and wrote. His works include several nonfiction books for children, novels, short stories, plays, operas and operettas, and newspaper columns.

Mr. Hughes was born on February 1, 1902 in Joplin, a small town in Missouri. His father, James Hughes, had studied law but because he was black he was refused the right to take his bar examination. Angry and fed up with Jim Crow society, he walked out of the house one day and went to Mexico.

Langston's childhood was spent shifting from one place to another, from relative to relative. He, too, suffered from racial discrimination. He attended Central High School in Cleveland, Ohio, and it was here that an English teacher, Miss Ethel Weimer, introduced him to some poetry by several new poets, including Carl Sandburg and Robert Frost. In his senior year, he was elected editor of the yearbook and class poet—an honor he earned by his contributions of poems to the school newspaper.

Upon graduation, Hughes went to visit his father. On the train heading south for Mexico, he created "The Negro Speaks of Rivers," a poem that became one of his best known compositions. He later sent the poem to Dr. W. E. B. DuBois, editor of *The Crisis* magazine. DuBois printed it; it was Hughes' first poem to appear in a magazine for adults. The following month "Aunt Sue's Stories" was published in *The Crisis*. The poem was written about his grandmother with whom he had lived and who died when he was twelve years old. *The Crisis* continued to publish his poetry. Hughes was soon to become known as the Black Poet Laureate.

In manhood, he began a series of wanderings across the world, visiting parts of Europe, Russia, and Africa, while working at a potpourri of jobs from dishwashing in a Parisian cafe to ranching on his father's ranch in Mexico.

His first book of poetry, *The Weary Blues,* was published in 1926 by Alfred A. Knopf. From this date on, his works regularly appeared in print, both poetry and prose. Hughes' creation, Jesse B. Semple (who became better known as Simple), was a philosophical character whose problems were typical of those faced by blacks.

Hughes completed his college education in 1929 when he graduated from Lincoln University, a college for black men in Pennsylvania. In later years, Hughes moved to Harlem and remained there until his death on May 27, 1967.

There are two excellent biographies of the poet that have recently been published: *Langston Hughes: A Biography,* (Crowell, 1968) by Milton Meltzer and *Black Troubador: Langston Hughes* by Charlemae H. Rollins (Rand-McNally, 1970).

Mr. Meltzer was a friend of Hughes and collaborated with him on two histories: *A Picture History of the Negro in America* (Crown, 1956, 1963) and *Black Magic: A Pictorial History of the Negro in American Entertainment* (Prentice-Hall, 1967). Mr. Meltzer's biography of the poet was a runner-up for the 1969 National Book Award.

Charlemae H. Rollins also knew the late poet. Her biography is illustrated with a variety of interesting photographs of Hughes, his family, friends, and several priceless reprints of letters, handwritten poems, and a facsimile of a Christmas card from "Simple." All of this adds greatly to the volume and gives a more personal impression of the poet. Lists of awards and honors, and the published works of Langston Hughes, are also included. The gifted poet Gwendolyn Brooks wrote the foreword.

Folkways/Scholastic Records has produced a classic recording, *The Dream Keeper and Other Poems,* featuring the late Langston Hughes reading selections for young people. Mr. Hughes shows how his poetry developed from specific experiences and ideas: A trip to the waterfront inspired "Waterfront

Streets"; from an old woman's memory of slavery, he created "Aunt Sue's Stories"; an idea that people should treasure their dreams became his famous poem, "Dreams." The soft, tender narrative provided by this master poet leads naturally into each of his selections, making the script biographic.

Caedmon Records has produced *The Poetry of Langston Hughes* featuring fifty poems read by Ruby Dee and Ossie Davis. This recording for mature listeners includes four of Hughes' "Madam" poems, his tribute "Frederick Douglass: 1817–1895," and "Juke Box Love Song." The record's sleeve includes excerpts from Arthur P. Davis' article, "The Harlem of Langston Hughes' Poetry," from the magazine, *Phylon: The Atlanta University Review of Race and Culture,* Fourth Quarter, 1952.

Hughes' work is widely anthologized. From personal experience I have found that his words are very meaningful to today's youth for in his poetry he spoke of the basic elements and emotions in life—love, hate, aspirations, despair; he wrote in the language of today and he does, and always will, speak for tomorrow.

While traveling around the country as a consultant to Bank Street College of Education, I had the opportunity to read this poet's works to students of various ages and backgrounds, from kindergarten classrooms to college campuses. Two years after the poet's death, I selected the poems that I had found were most meaningful to children. The result is the collection of forty-five Hughes poems in *Don't You Turn Back* (Alfred A. Knopf, 1969), illustrated with strong, bold two-color woodcuts by Ann Grifalconi. The text is divided into four sections: "My People," "Prayers and Dreams," "Out to Sea," and "I, Too, Am a Negro." The poems represent a wide range of Hughes' work—from his first published poem, "The Negro Speaks of Rivers," to "Color," which appeared in *The Panther and the Lash* (Alfred A. Knopf, 1967), published after the poet's death.

Many eulogies were written about the poet and his contributions to American literature. Perhaps the most tender one was one created by a fourth-grade Harlem girl who knew and loved his work. She wrote this poem the day after Hughes died.

In Memorium to Langston Hughes
The Useless Pen

A pen lay useless on the desk.
A mother once held a babe on her breast.
Where is the lad this very day?
Down by Poetry Bay they say,
Where the Poets sit and think all day
Of a way to make people happy.
Even though they are not here today
I know they meet by Poetry Bay
Trying to think of a special way
To welcome Langston to Poetry Bay.

MARY O'NEILL

Mary O'Neill was raised in what she has described as a wonderful barn of a Victorian house in Berea, Ohio. She was educated at Our Lady of Lourdes Academy, St. Joseph's Academy, Western Reserve University, and the University of Michigan. She entered the advertising field and after becoming a partner in her own advertising agency, she moved to New York City where she now lives. She is the mother of three children and the grandmother of several.

Mrs. O'Neill's first book for children is the popular collection *Hailstones and Halibut Bones: Adventures in Color*

(Doubleday, 1961), which explores in poems the spectrum of different colors. Her poetry has been used with children of all ages to spark them into seeing color in new ways (see chapter 3 for ideas on how to use these poems in the classroom). Her rhyming poems not only let us see colors but hear them, touch them, smell, and taste them. She tells us such things as "Time is purple," "Brown is chocolate/And gingerbread," and "You can hear blue/In wind over water."

In recent years, several of the poems in her book have caused a bit of controversy when I've introduced them to graduate students. Some students have objected to images such as "Red is an Indian," or the color black being "things you'd like to forget," or "Black is a feeling/Hard to explain/Like suffering but/Without the pain." These examples should not deter teachers from using the book, however. Discussing these images with children can provoke interesting discussions.

The text of *Hailstones...* is illustrated by the Caldecott Award winning artist Leonard Weisgard. A film of the same title is also available. Six poems are read by Celeste Holm against a cartoon-like animated background.

In *People I'd Like to Keep* (Doubleday, 1963), the poet offers engaging looks at fifteen people including "The Balloon Man," "The Circus People," and "Uggle," not a person but a blanket worn to shreds which is "Like somebody, almost,/But not quite..." Illustrations for the text were done by Paul Galdone.

Words, Words, Words (Doubleday, 1966) is a book of verses telling how words started, where they have come from through the ages, and the rules we follow when putting them together. Here is a text that perfectly ties in with language arts and social studies lessons. Included are: "Nobody Knows What the First Words Were," "Egyptian Hieroglyphic Writing," and poems that teach what sentences, phrases, parts of speech, and certain letters of the alphabet are all about. Poems about specific words also appear: "Goosebeery," "Fascination," and "Felicity." The book is decorated with drawings by Judy Piussi-Campbell.

What Is That Sound? (Atheneum, 1966) is an onomatopoeia-trip where a fire hisses, crackles, pops, whooshes and snaps; and where water gurgles, splashes, crashes, murmurs, ripples, and roars. This is another book that is a lively springboard to creative writing.

In *Take a Number* (Doubleday, 1968) the poet combines the lilt and rhythm of poetry with the language of mathematics. She deals with specific numbers and number concepts—addition, subtraction, and the history of numbers. The book is illustrated by Al Nagy.

Various kinds of fingers are the subject of *Fingers Are Always Bringing Me News* (Doubleday, 1969)—newborn fingers, children's fingers, city and country fingers, greedy fingers, and the fingers of Mimi, a blind child. Drawings for the text are by Don Bolognese.

Many of Mrs. O'Neill's poems are long and made up of short lyrical lines. Her poetry speaks to children and excites them to look at familiar things around them in new and fresh ways. Having all her books on hand is like having a treasure chest of verse, for her poems fit neatly into nearly every part of the school curriculum. Many of them can be shared with children in lower grades, but they are most effective when used with girls and boys in the upper-elementary grades. Recently, the poet created her first book for very young readers, *Big Red Hen,* (Doubleday, 1971).

Mrs. O'Neill's work can best be summed up by a fifth-grade teacher with whom I worked who stated, "My children didn't seem to enjoy poetry until I, and they, found Mary O'Neill. Now we're all hooked!"

THEODORE ROETHKE

Theodore Roethke (*roth-key*) was born on May 25, 1908, in Saginaw, Michigan. His father ran a large greenhouse in the Saginaw Valley behind which were swamps, forests, and wild game preserves. Roethke has recalled: "It was a wonderful place for a child to grow up in and around. Ever since I could walk, I have spent as much time as I could in the open. I have a genuine love of nature."

His first book of poems for adults, *Open House* (Alfred A. Knopf), was published in 1941; in 1953 he won the coveted Pulitzer Prize for Poetry for *The Waking: Poems 1933–1953* (Doubleday). Roethke looked for a sense of self by creating poetry from childhood memories. His father's greenhouse sparked him to write a great deal about nature and art. He has said, "I write only about people and things that I know thoroughly."

An excellent collection to acquaint boys and girls with the poet's work is *I Am! Says the Lamb* (Doubleday, 1961). This book, put together for children in the upper grades, has two sections: the first contains many of his nature poems; the second his humorous poetry. To truly make children Roethke fans there is an exciting seven-inch LP record entitled *The Light and Serious Side of Theodore Roethke* (available from Scholastic Book Services). This recording contains fifteen poems, several read by the poet himself. Side 1, "The Light Side," features ten poems including his renowned "The Lizard," "Myrtle" (a most intelligent turtle), and his limerick "Philander." Side 2, "The Serious Side," features five poems including "Night Journey," and "Elegy for Jane: My Student Thrown by a Horse," which appears in his Pulitzer Prize winning book. Roethke recorded these poems at the University of Washington in Seattle where he taught shortly before his death on August 1, 1963.

In recent years, Roethke's poems have been anthologized in several popular books of poems. "The Bat" and "The Heron" are included in Nancy Larrick's anthology *Piping Down the Valleys Wild* (Delacorte, 1968; also available in paperback from Dell); "The Sloth" appears in the picture book *A Paper Zoo: A Collection of Animal Poems by Modern American Poets* (Atheneum, 1968) selected by Renée Karol Weiss. *Roethke: Collected Poems* (Doubleday, 1966) contains 200 of the poet's works, many of which will have special appeal to children in the upper-elementary grades.

CARL SANDBURG

Carl Sandburg was one of those rare poetic geniuses. He was the son of two poor Swedish immigrants and was born on January 6, 1878, in Galesburg, Illinois, a city about 145 miles southwest of Chicago in Abraham Lincoln country. During his lifetime he worked as a laborer, secretary, newspaperman, political organizer, historian, lecturer, and collector and singer of folksongs. He frequently toured the United States with his guitar singing folksongs and reciting his poems.

Thirty years of his life were spent preparing a monumental six-volume biography of Lincoln; in 1940 he was awarded the Pulitzer Prize in History for the last four volumes, *Abraham Lincoln: The War Years* (1939; unless otherwise noted, all of Sandburg's books were published by Harcourt). In 1950, he received a second Pulitzer Prize, this time for his *Complete Poems*.

A great deal has been written about this poet. In 1969 the Library of Congress prepared an eighty-three-page pamphlet entitled *Carl Sandburg* (U.S. Government Printing Office), which includes an essay by Mark Van Doren and sixty-five pages listing Sandburg materials in the collection at the Library of Congress.

Sandburg's first published work appeared in 1904, *In Reckless Ecstasy*. Only fifty copies were printed by one of Sandburg's professors, Phillip Green Wright, who owned and operated a printing press in Galesburg. Three other volumes of his work were printed between 1907–1910. In 1914 Harriet Monroe, who was editor of the avant-garde *Poetry: A Magazine of Verse,* received a group of nine poems from Sandburg. They shocked her. They were unlike anything she was used to reading and/or receiving. Among the nine poems were the now famous, widely anthologized, "Chicago," which has become a staple in American literature. This poem, along with the eight others, was included in his first book, *Chicago Poems* (Holt, Rinehart and Winston, 1916), a book reflecting the tempo, life, and language of the everyday people whom Sandburg encountered. Following this volume, Sandburg's writings were published at a rapid pace; *Cornhuskers,* his last poetry book for Holt (1918), *Smoke and Steel* (1920), his writings about Lincoln, his famous *Rootabaga* stories for children, and his poetry for children *Early Moon* (1930) and *Wind Song* (1960; also available in paperback).

The best volume for use with children in the elementary grades appeared in 1970. *The Carl Sandburg Treasury: Prose and Poetry for Young People* includes the complete *Rootabaga Stories, Abraham Lincoln Grows Up, Prairie Town Boy, Early Moon,* and *Wind Song.* The introduction is written by his wife, Paula.

Early Moon begins with Sandburg's must-read "Short Talk on Poetry," a beautiful essay explaining "how little anybody knows about poetry, how it is made, what it is made of, how long men have been making it, where it came from, when it began, who started it and why, and who knows all about it." The text contains many of his widely anthologized poems that children love including "Phizzog,"—"this face you got"—"Buffalo Dusk," "Manual System" and "Fog" which appears just about everywhere!

Wind Song contains his much loved poems "Arithmetic," "Paper I" and "Paper II," several of his "Margaret" poems, written for his daughter, and "Circles," a seven-line free verse that beautifully sums up the white man's ignorance of the unknown as pointed out by an Indian.

Works of Sandburg appear in nearly every major anthology of children's poetry. His words are as fresh today as they were fifty years ago and will continue to be years hence.

Mature readers will enjoy reading the biography *Carl Sandburg, Yes,* by W. G. Rogers (Harcourt, 1970). Two recordings of Sandburg reading his own work are available from Caedmon (distributed by D. C. Heath): *Poems for Children,* which includes Sandburg's discussion of poetry for children and the poems "Buffalo Dusk," "Phizzog," and "Arithmetic" among others: and *Carl Sandburg Reading Fog and Other Poems* includes "Wind Song," "Wilderness," "River Moon," and twenty-five other selections.

The poet died on July 22, 1967, at the age of eighty-nine. On his death President Lyndon Baines Johnson issued the statement:

Carl Sandburg needs no epitaph. It is written for all time in the fields, the cities, the face, and heart of the land he loved and the people he celebrated and inspired. With the world we mourn his passing. It is our pride and fortune as Americans that we will always hear Carl Sandburg's voice within ourselves. For he gave us the truest and most enduring vision of our own greatness.

Sandburg's birthplace, 331 East 3rd Street in Galesburg, Illinois, still stands as a monument to the poet. Each year approximately 15,000 adults and children visit this memorial to Illinois' poet laureate.

The preceding discussions have been limited primarily to volumes of original verse. The elementary classroom should contain many such volumes along with a number of poetry anthologies. Using anthologies is an excellent way to acquaint boys and girls with a variety of poets and their different writing styles, and they are convenient to have on hand for children and teachers to dip into whenever they feel the need. One of the greatest benefits of a good anthology is that its poems can satisfy many interests and levels and are balanced with work by poets of all genres.

Good anthologists strive for this variety. The children's anthologist William Cole wittily remarked to me that, "Any anthology done without enthusiasm is like a TV dinner—frozen, tasteless, and quickly forgotten."

Anthologies can be grouped in two categories: (1) general anthologies that contain poems on nearly any subject, sometimes grouped or arranged under specific topics and (2) specialized anthologies that contain poems on a particular subject.

Every classroom should have a potpourri of poetry on its bookshelves. Collections of original verse and general and specialized anthologies should be present in number. One good anthology isn't enough! With many high quality anthologies available both in hardcover and paperbound editions, the class can enjoy the hundreds of poems and poets tucked inside several volumes. Librarians or booksellers can suggest the more popular anthologies for use in your classroom. But before you choose or buy, decide for *yourself* what is best for you and your students.

FOR FURTHER READING

Alexander, Arthur. *The Poet's Eye: An Introduction to Poetry for Young People.* Englewoods Cliffs, N.J.: Prentice-Hall, 1967.

A fine introduction to poetry written for older students. "A Glossary of Poetic Terms" is included defining meter, figures of speech, and poetic sound. The text is sometimes over-detailed but good for serious students who want to delve into the study and creation of various poem schemes.

Baring-Gould, William S. and Ceil, eds. *The Annotated Mother Goose.* New York: Meridian Books, 1967; also available in paperback.

This book, for teacher's reference or use with children in upper-elementary grades, contains hundreds of old and new nursery rhymes with scholarly explanations. The book contains black and white illustrations by artists such as Kate Greenaway, Randolph Caldecott, and Walter Crane, along with historical woodcuts. It is one of the best reference collections available. Chapter I tells "All about 'Mother Goose' verses that have become the beloved heritage of nobody-really knows when and where."

Behn, Harry. "Poetry, Fantasy and Reality," *Elementary English,* April 1965, pp. 355–61.

In this address presented during the National Council of Teachers of English Convention in Cleveland, Ohio, 1964, Mr. Behn discusses how he began to write for children and presents some of his views on poetry and children.

———. "Poetry for Children," *Horn Book,* April 1966, pp. 163–75.

The poet speaks on poetry revealing a great deal about himself, the poetry he writes, and the children for whom it is intended.

Clark, Leonard. "Poetry for the Youngest," *Horn Book,* December 1962, pp. 582–5.

The author makes a plea for getting poetry into children's lives as early as possible. His philosophy is summed up in this quotation: ". . . it is wise to remember that it matters much more for the child if the greater emphasis is laid on the way the words in the poems *sound* rather than on what the words *say*."

Diffin, Leslye T. "Opening the Door to Poetry," *The Instructor,* October 1966, p. 34.

Poetry used creatively in the primary and early middle grades is presented.

Hopkins, Lee Bennett, *Books Are by People: Interviews with 104 Authors and Illustrators of Books for Young Children.* New York: Citation Press, 1969; also available in paperback.

Lively, personal interviews with such noted poets as David McCord, Dr. Seuss, Eve Merriam, Myra Cohn Livingston, and Aileen Fisher are included as well as anthologists Sara and John E. Brewton, William Cole, and Richard Lewis. Interviews contain vignettes of poets' lives, their views on poetry, and the trials and tribulations of writing verse for boys and girls.

Lanes, Selma G. *Down the Rabbit Hole: Adventures and Misadventures in the Realm of Children's Literature.* New York: Atheneum, 1971.

In chapter six, "Seuss For the Goose is Seuss for the Gander," the author cites the value of bringing up children on Seussian characters. She states: "We not only get our money's worth, but are left with a reservoir of sane thoughts and an appetite for his next outlandish invention. Long live Theodor Seuss Geisel, physician to the psyche of the beleaguered modern child!"

Livingston, Myra Cohn. "Not the Rose. . . ." *Horn Book,* August 1964. pp. 355–360.

Mrs. Livingston discusses the importance of poetry, sharing her views and confirming the fact that poetry cannot be explained or proved or rationalized or classified. It is personal—bringing to life a discovery that man is one with the world, part of the great beauty and harmony of the universe.

Mother Goose. *The Original Mother Goose's Melody as First Issued by John Newbery of London, about A.D., 1760. Reproduced in Fac-similie from the Edition as Reprinted by Isaiah Thomas, of Worcester, Mass. about A.D., 1785, with Introduc-*

tory Notes by William H. Whitmore. Albany: Joel Munsell's Sons, 1889; Detroit: The Singing Tree Press, a division of Gale Research Company, 1969.

This delightful volume is one that will have special appeal to teachers. Whitmore's introductory notes thoroughly discuss the origin, development, and popularity of Mother Goose rhymes and provide a history of the publication of various editions.

Stewart-Gordon, James. "Dr. Seuss: Fanciful Sage of Childhood." *Reader's Digest,* April 1972, pp. 141–145.

A fine and lively article discussing "this magician of the imagination," his life, and works.

From *Don't Tell the Scarecrow and Other Japanese Poems*. Copyright © 1969 by Talivaldis Stubis. Used by permission of Four Winds Press, a division of Scholastic Magazines, Inc.

"BUTTERFLIES CAN BE IN BELLIES!"

SPARKING CHILDREN TO WRITE POETRY

Once children have been exposed to and enjoyed poetry over a period of time, they will naturally react to an offer to compose poems of their own. Recently many anthologies (see Appendix II) have appeared containing good verse by children—ample evidence of their ability to create and appreciate poetry.

In 1966, when Richard Lewis' *Miracles: Poems by Children of the English Speaking World* (Simon and Schuster) was published, the world was treated to a fresh glimpse of how children can write and what they write about. Mr. Lewis visited eighteen countries where English was either the native tongue or an important second language. In the "Introductory Note" to his book, he states:

Whatever the circumstances, wherever I went . . . I found that, given the right encouragement and understanding, children could and did write poems that invited serious attention *as poetry*. Indeed, the children's very limitations of vocabulary and grammar served much the same function as the deliberate restrictions of form that the adult poet uses to concentrate his vision.

In this treasure house of poems, still one of the best volumes of children's writings, girls and boys spill out thoughts and images about seasons, play, people, feelings—and poetry, too! Leafing through this volume one sees childhood in all its forms

—uncertainty, fear, joy, anxiety about growing up, love, and most importantly, being a child. A Caedmon recording of *Miracles* is available from D. C. Heath and Company; Julie Harris and Roddy McDowell read the poems.

Children can write poetry and should. Poetry by children is meant to be shared, and it can be in an endless variety of ways. Children can read their works to one another, print it in a class or school newspaper, include it in a play or assembly program, or give it as a priceless gift to someone special.

Too often I receive letters from teachers, librarians, and parents asking me how they can get Charlie's poem published. The important thing to Charlie should be the creation of something from within himself—and that is enough! A child's poem is not any better because it appears in print. We must not feel that everything a child writes must be published. Children's poems do not have to appear in a published work to be good, to be enjoyed by oneself, one's peers, or by an intimate group. The thing teachers should do most is encourage children to write, to play around with language, use words in new and special ways, and develop their creative potential.

Poetry is not easy to write. Children should be taught to create a composition, re-work it and re-work it again, until they feel it is perfect. One way to start children off is to begin with a simple language device such as the simile.

SIMILES

Using similes is a good method of introducing children to ways of coloring their thoughts. Similes are figures of speech that compare two dissimilar objects using *like* or *as*.

Give children phrases such as "As green as ———" and

ask them to fill in their immediate response. When I suggest this at workshops, I ask the audience to give *their* response. Immediately a chorus chants, "As green as *grass!*"

Laughingly, I tell the audience that if their first-, third- or fifth-grade youngsters said that, they would call them *uncreative!* Yet, this a perfect response. What is greener than grass? To a child "tired answers" are really quite fresh since everyday brings new experiences, new reactions, and quite naturally the repetition of many responses we, ourselves, had as children. To encourage other responses, you can ask the children to look around the classroom for things that are green. Mary's dress, for example, might have green on it; Donald's notebook might be green; the chalkboard may be green; Sharon's pocketbook might have shades of green in it. Thus, children begin to see the many uses of the color green and develop broader perspectives.

Now that they have seen green in the classroom, ask, "What else is green?" Allow the children to brainstorm until they have exhausted the possibilities. Then try another simile using something other than color, for example, "as big as ————," "as tired as ————," or as *anything* as.

Great results should not be expected the first few times around, but great results can be elicited when girls and boys get and develop the idea that things can be poetically compared via the use of similes.

From the *as* or *like* phrases, lead the children into other comparisons: "The house was as ———— as ————," "The rain was like ————," or "The book was like ————."

Third-graders have said:

The mouse is as small as my hand was the day I was born.

The giant in the fairy tale is as tall as Wilt Chamberlain.

The lady is as roly-poly as Santa Claus' Jello stomach.

This, then, is a small beginning to start children thinking in terms of poetic imagery and finally to setting their thoughts down in pint-sized poems.

In a short but pointed article, "Age and Grade Expectancy in Poetry: Maturity in Self-Expression" (*Today's Catholic Teacher,* September 12, 1969, pp. 18–9), Nina Willis Walter discusses the fact that a child's first attempts at writing poetry are usually very simple and that even a student in high school who has not previously attempted a poem may begin to express himself at a very elementary level of writing. She reports:

The comparison of snow to a blanket is not new, but the following poem was a creative effort for the child who wrote it because the idea of making comparisons was new to him and because he was looking at the snow and saying what it looked like to him.

> The snow
> Is like a big white blanket
> On the ground
> —Joey Barnes, age 6

Rather than dismissing Joey's composition as *uncreative,* it would be better to develop with him additional ideas of snow, using other similes and leading him into metaphors—figures of speech in which one thing is likened to another, for example, William Shakespeare's, "All the world's a stage..."

SHORT-VERSE FORMS

Teachers across the country have successfully used short verse forms to call forth novel thoughts from young minds. The more popular short verse-forms that can be used in the elementary classroom include haiku, senryu, and tanka stemming from the ancient Japanese culture, sijo from Korea, and the cinquain and diamante forms originated in twentieth century America.

HAIKU

In recent years haiku has been read and written coast-to-coast in classrooms from grades one through six. There are many reasons for this successful use of haiku with children—the poems are short, and the form is easy to remember and construct.

The form was invented in Japan centuries ago; it consists of only three non-rhyming lines, containing seventeen syllables, five-seven-five respectively. (Naturally, since the Japanese language differs from English, this form is changed when original Japanese haiku is translated.)

The basic requirement of the form is that, in some way, the haiku should relate to nature or the seasons of the year. A good haiku should be able to tell the reader approximately the season from certain key words that appear within the seventeen syllables.

Another requirement is that the haiku capture a moment or a single image in the busy world of nature. A haiku poem should strike an image almost as if a slide were flashed upon a screen in a darkened room.

Children of all ages can try their hand at creating haiku, concentrating and writing about a brief moment; no child, however, should be forced into the five-seven-five syllable limitations. I recently received a letter from a fifth-grade child from Whitehall, Michigan, who was puzzled over the poem "Hokku: In the Falling Snow" by Richard Wright that is included in *Faces and Places: Poems for You* (Scholastic Book

Services, 1971). The child was puzzled and concerned because the poem contains eight syllables in the second line instead of the "required" seven. The required form should be suggested to students, but not enforced. The world will not be shattered if Mr. Wright's haiku, or any child's, contains eighteen syllables or fifteen! The point is to motivate children to express themselves in a few words and decide which words he can use to communicate his idea poetically.

Janet Glickman, a teacher in the Stephen Decatur School in Philadelphia, reports on "A First Grade Haiku Project" (*Elementary English,* February 1970, pp. 265–6). She read her class haiku and discussed it to acquaint the children with this type of poetry. She then taught the form and worked with the children until each had written at least one haiku poem. The finished products were compiled into a booklet, duplicated, and given to each class member. Mrs. Glickman also had the children tape their poems as an additional bonus activity.

No matter in what grade you introduce this form, it is wise to read to the class a variety of haiku that pinpoints the qualities of the poems. There are many excellent volumes of haiku poetry. Among the best and most popular for reading aloud and use by children themselves are the following:

Caudill, Rebecca. *Come Along.* New York: Holt, Rinehart and Winston, 1969.

This collection of original haiku verse is beautifully illustrated in rich full-color by Ellen Raskin. Miss Raskin has commented, "I wanted the reader to see beyond the boundaries of the book as I tried to compliment the author's word images with acrylic paint on colored rice paper . . . I have hoped to achieve not a picture of a landscape, but, like the haiku, a moment in nature."

Issa. *A Few Flies and I.* Selected by Jean Merrill and Ronnie Solbert. New York: Pantheon, 1969.

The haiku in this collection were all written by the Japanese poet, Issa, born over two hundred years ago. Each page of this handsome volume is tenderly illustrated in oriental fashion by Ronnie Solbert.

Issa, Yayū, Kikaku, and other Japanese poets. *Don't Tell the Scarecrow.* New York: Four Winds Press, 1969; also available in paperback from Scholastic Book Services.

A collection of astutely selected haiku relevant to a child and his world. Much of the success of this book is due to the artistry of Tālavaldis Stubis; his soft, evocative illustrations compliment each of the poems and provide a magic touch in which children will delight.

Johnson, Hannah Lyons. *Hello, Small Sparrow.* New York: Lothrop, Lee and Shepard, 1971.

The poet has taken "poetic license" and has written her haiku verse in seventeen syllables using four lines instead of the popular three. The rich, exciting illustrations done both in black and white and full color by Tony Chen add greatly to this collection of original verse that will have special appeal to very young boys and girls.

Lewis, Richard, ed. *In a Spring Garden.* New York: Dial Press, 1965.

The verse in this volume follows a day of spring from the early morning admonition to a toad who "looks as if/It would belch forth/A cloud" to the glowing goodnight of a firefly. The master artist Ezra Jack Keats provides perfect collage illustrations to compliment this volume.

—————, ed. *The Moment of Wonder.* New York: Dial Press, 1964.

A rich collection of Chinese and Japanese poetry. Many haiku poems are included as well as simple three-line verses that lightly sketch a scene, mood, or image. The text is illustrated by Chinese and Japanese artists. This volume is particularly suited for older girls and boys.

————, ed. *Of This World: A Poet's Life in Poetry.* New York: Dial Press, 1968.

In this volume Mr. Lewis has created a biography of Issa, one of the most famous of the haiku poets, who was born on the Day of the Iris Festival in 1763. The book is illustrated with striking black and white photographs by Helen Buttfield.

A teacher can find many volumes explaining the haiku form for his own reference. The best of the lot is a compact paperbound volume, *Haiku in English* (Charles E. Tuttle Company, 1967), by Harold G. Henderson. This book explains everything you will need to know, gives many examples of haiku by master poets, and suggests lesson plans. The volume is one that every teacher should have tucked inside a pocket or pocketbook, ready to be pulled out at a second's notice.

To motivate one lesson in writing haiku, I did the following. I brought to a fifth-grade class a bunch of jonquils and placed them in a clear vase filled with water. Alongside the vase I placed a mason jar containing a live bumblebee (caught by one of the students in the class, not by me!). This was done prior to the 8:45 admission bell. Several children, upon entering the classroom, noticed the fresh flowers and the bee on my desk. Other children came in and went to their desks without bothering to look at my Tuesday morning display. But as with any group of fifth-graders, contagious behavior is as normal as adults having coffee with breakfast. Soon there was more buzzing in the classroom than any group of healthy bees could have produced. When the entire class was settled, I asked them to look at and concentrate on the flowers and the bumblebee for just three minutes (which can be a long, long time for thirty curious creators). I told them to look at the flowers and bee as they never looked at anything before. At the end of three minutes, I carried the jar to the window, dramatically opened it, and sent Mr. Bumblebee off to freedom. I then asked the class to think about the entire experience—looking at the flowers and the caged-up bee and my letting the bee go free. Now the children were ready to write haiku. I had provided them with nature, a moment, and an image. Then they were free to write. And they did!

James wrote:

> The bee is jailed.
> Never again will he taste
> The flowers he loves.

Freida and Harriet wrote:

> The bee is set free
> But flowers, you'll only stay
> Alive for a while.

> Yellow bee. Go to
> The yellow flowers outside
> Where you both are free.

Many simple objects from nature might be used to stimulate young minds—a twig, a rock, a cricket, or a bunch of leaves. With the great emphasis on ecology today, haiku is a natural tie-in. Many haiku poems written by great masters centuries ago are more relevant today than they might have been at the time they were written. One such example written by Issa, appears in *Don't Tell the Scarecrow:*

> Little knowing
> The tree will soon be cut down,
> Birds are building their nests in it.

Another way to motivate children after they have read or heard a lot of haiku in English is to show them non-print media. Often a film or sound filmstrip can provide many ideas to spark children's thoughts. Also, since haiku deals with nature, children in all parts of the country can partake in new experiences. Few children in Louisiana, for example, have ever seen a snowfall or a frozen brook melting to help spring come about; many city girls and boys may never know what it is like to roam through the countryside discovering wildflowers or fiddle-head ferns. The magic of media can allow children to experience things they never have experienced directly. Some of the best written work is often produced because new images have been flashed before children's eyes.

There are three excellent films to use with elementary school children: *Haiku: An Introduction to Poetry,* distributed by Coronet Films, *A Day Is Two Feet Long* and *In a Spring Garden,* the latter two distributed by Weston Woods.

Haiku: An Introduction to Poetry is a beautiful film depicting man's relationship to his environment. Kiu Haghaghi, a composer and musician from Iran, plays the sitar giving the film an added dimension. Haiku verses are expertly woven into the sound track.

A Day Is Two Feet Long is a live-action film that attempts to create visually the haiku experience. The sound track consists only of natural sounds—water rushing over rocks, winds blowing, birds chirping. The work was conceived and directed by Peter Rubin, a filmmaker and lecturer on films. A promotion piece about the film contains four "reviews" from sixth-grade students in Kokomo, Indiana. The children stated:

I had the feeling that I was alone in the world with nature.

It made me feel as if I was just waking up.

Everything seemed to be just born.

I felt the world desolate.

Every child and adult will have something to say and to think about after viewing this most unusual film.

In a Spring Garden, based upon the book of the same title, is available as both a six-minute film and as a filmstrip-book-record combination. Both media are narrated by Richard Lewis, editor of the volume, and both are excellent. Personally, I have found the filmstrip package more successful for use with children in elementary grades. You can show one, two, or several frames, allow the children to savor the exquisite collage images created by Ezra Jack Keats, and read them the accompanying verse yourself. The film is rather fast-paced, and very young children will lose the mood you are trying to set by seeing too much all at once.

Another source of inspiration is a magnificent portfolio of eleven reproductions of works by master Japanese artists distributed by Shorewood Reproductions, Inc. The reproductions are large, suitable for framing, and include works such as Sekkyo's "Bull," Kiyonga's "Woman Under a Window," and Koryusai's "Winter Autumn."

With the portfolio is a teaching guide containing aims and giving many excellent suggestions for using the prints to spark the writing of haiku poetry. The entire kit is contained in a handsome fireboard permanent storage file. A better value cannot be found.

SENRYU

Senryu, another popular verse form, is related to haiku. Senryu, named for the Japanese poet who originated the form, follows the same five-seven-five pattern of haiku and also concentrates on a single idea or image of a moment. The form differs in that the subject matter is not restricted to nature nor to the seasons. This form gives a child the opportunity to express his ideas on any subject—baseball, eating spaghetti, or camping out in the woods. Below are two examples of senryu;

the first was created by a second-grade child, the second by a fifth-grader:

> The first day of school.
> Now I know that butterflies
> Can be in bellies.

> Nothing is better
> Than baseball, except maybe
> Football, or soccer.

TANKA

Tanka are longer in form and again typically deal with nature or a season of the year. Tanka is written in five lines of thirty-one syllables, five-seven-five-seven-seven respectively. The first three lines are known as the *hokku;* the last two, the *ageku.* Older girls and boys will enjoy experimenting with the tanka form after they have been introduced to and mastered the haiku. A rich resource of tanka poetry can be found in *The Seasons of Time: Poetry of Ancient Japan* (Dial, 1968) edited by Virginia Baron Olsen. The poetry in this collection was originally commissioned by the Emperor of Japan and was written by poets, priests, warriors, and courtiers. The text, beautifully illustrated in brush and ink calligraphy by Yashuhide Kobashi, is excellent to use with children.

SIJO

The sijo (shē-jo) verse form is a product of the fourteenth century Yi Dynasty of Korea. This period in Korean history was a sort of Renaissance during which science, industry, literature, and the arts developed rapidly.

The form is similar to the haiku in several ways: it is based on syllabication, it is unrhymed, and it usually deals with nature or the seasons. In English the form is written in six lines, each line containing seven or eight syllables, with a total of forty-two to forty-eight syllables.

During one very hot summer, while working with a group of children in a Title III program in Hartford, Connecticut, I introduced the sijo form. When I asked what the group would like to write about, two replies came simultaneously: "Somethin' cold," said one child; another replied, "Old Man Winter!" Thus, thoughts of winter were conjured up in sijo form while we all melted away. One child produced the following:

> Winter is a God-given gift:
> It's a pretty good one too!
>   To see the white flakes falling
>   And cold, cold wind a-blowin'
> Life seems like the seasons
> Changing with no reasons.

A boy in the group wrote this imaginative piece:

> What a gloomy, snowy night.
> Dull, moody, all the way.
> The ship's crew are all in fright...
> The choppy waves roll off the coast...
> In the galley, pots are rattling.
> Storm-stopped ships on their way.

One of my favorite compositions came out of this session. It was created by two Spanish-speaking boys with a paucity of English vocabulary. They wrote:

> We like to see how machines work
> Me and my good friend José Rosa.
> The old pieces are all black.

The dirt goes to our fingernails
And the oil goes to our pants.
We have to use big and small tools.

In Harlem, a sixth-grade unit on Korea incorporated the sijo form. One boy wrote:

I wonder what it's like to
Be a crawling caterpillar.
They're always so alone
And ugly and without friends, and sad . . .
But when the time comes
Everyone is fooled—a butterfly is born!

Again, it must be emphasized that the strict form should not be a deterrent for children. In the examples provided above, you will note that the seven-to-eight-syllable count per line does vary now and then. Other examples of children's sijo may be found in my article "Sijo" (*The Instructor*, March 1969, pp. 76–7).

There are two excellent resources for teachers containing examples of sijo translated from the original Korean by Peter H. Lee: *Anthology of Korean Poetry* (John Day Company, 1964) and *Korean Literature: Themes and Topics,* (University of Arizona Press, 1965). Children will enjoy listening to and reading many of the selections contained within these volumes.

CINQUAIN

I was first introduced to the cinquain form when visiting Frances Weissman's fourth-grade class in East Paterson, New Jersey. I immediately became fascinated with both the form and the creations that the boys and girls in the class were producing.

Cinquain is a delicately compressed, five line, unrhymed stanza containing twenty-two syllables broken into a two-four-six-eight-two pattern. The form was originated by Adelaide Crapsey, who was born on September 9, 1878, in Brooklyn Heights, New York.

Miss Crapsey studied at Kemper Hall in Kenosha, Wisconsin and after graduating from Vassar College in 1901, she returned to Kemper Hall to teach. In 1905 she went to Rome to study archeology. She remained in Italy for one year and returned to teach at Miss Low's Preparatory School for Girls in Stamford, Connecticut (now the Low-Heywood School for girls in grades six through twelve). The remainder of her life she fought a losing battle against tuberculosis.

The years 1913–1914 were spent in a sanatorium in Saranac, New York; it was here, in a room that faced an old, sadly abandoned graveyard, that she wrote and perfected cinquains. Miss Crapsey termed this plot of land "Trudeau's Garden," after Edward Livingston Trudeau, an American physician who pioneered open-air treatment for tuberculosis at Saranac. This view, plus her prolonged illness, probably inspired her to write verses, both cinquain and other poetic forms, about death. One of the longest poems was titled "To the Dead in My Graveyard Underneath My Window." This poem was published in 1915, a year after her death, in a slender collection of her work simply titled *Verse*.

In his preface to the 1938 edition of *Verse* (Knopf), Carl Bragdon wrote of Miss Crapsey: "I remember her as fair and fragile, in action swift, in repose still; so quick and silent in her movements that she seemed never to enter a room but to appear there, and on the stroke of some invisible clock to vanish as she had come."

In my travels around the country, I have introduced this

form to many children. Samples are published in my book *City Talk* (Knopf, 1970). Below are two selections:

> Two days
> Which are special—
> Yes! One is my birthday
> And one belongs to Abe, my friend,
> Who's dead.
> > —Michael de Veaux

> One day
> A horse ran fast
> He ran so fast that wind,
> Sunlight, and all the blue of day
> Flew gone!
> > —Wilfred Horne, Jr.

Like the other verse forms discussed, the cinquain allows the child to spontaneously put forth his or her thoughts and feelings in a minimum number of words and lines. Again, the children's writings should not necessarily have to conform to the formula; over-stepping the structured boundaries often enables girls and boys to write more freely.

DIAMANTE

Iris M. Tiedt, an assistant professor at the University of Santa Clara, Santa Clara, California, introduced a new form of poetry in an article "A New Poetic Form: The Diamante" (*Elementary English,* May, 1969, pp. 588–9). She invented the diamante (dee-ah-*mahn*-tay) while searching for varied ways to stimulate poetry writing by youngsters. Poems are created using seven lines forming a diamond pattern. They are contrast poems following these specifications:

Line 1—one word, subject noun
Line 2—two adjectives
Line 3—three participles (either -ing, -ed, but not a mixture)
Line 4—four nouns related to the subject
Line 5—three participles
Line 6—two adjectives
Line 7—one noun opposite of the subject

Rhyme and rhythm are not needed, but naturally children must know their parts of speech very well. Obviously diamante should be reserved for children who will not be intimidated by its scholarly requirements. Presenting this type of poetic form to an unprepared child can quite easily negate much of the value that poetry holds.

Here is one example of the diamante, written by a sixth-grade child in Hartford, Connecticut:

Cat
Soft, cuddly
Purring, scratching, playing
Baby, kitten, change, adult
Lurking, leaping, killing
Meaner, madder
Tiger.

Note that the fourth line marks the transition to the opposite idea. The words here reflect the transformation from *cat* to *tiger*. Lines 5, 6, and 7 develop the contrasting figure.

In her article Mrs. Tiedt gives three examples: diamantes contrasting child to adult, country to city, and sea to land. There are endless possibilities for children to write about; war to peace, school to vacation, or summer to fall are several topics they might like to explore.

The interesting thing about the form is that children must carefully think of the words they choose.

In all these short verse forms, children can write, experiment, and perfect poetic imagery. And through short verse forms a child can play on city streets, bask in the beauty of the country-side or even go to Neverland Land, as it was called by a child from Julesburg, Colorado.

JAPANESE CLASSIFICATIONS OF BEAUTY

Before or after boys and girls have experimented with and created short verse forms, have them try their hands at form-ing word-pictures using the four Japanese classifications of beauty: (1) *Hade* (ha-day), (2) *Iki* (ē-kee), (3) *Jimi* (jē-mē), and (4), *Shibui* (shē-bu-ē). There is no particular form for children to follow as in the above short verse forms. The idea is to have children evoke strong imagery through word-thoughts. Children can experiment with the arrangement of words to give their images a more poetic look.

Hade signifies something that is colorful, flashy, or bright, for example:

> The signs on 42nd Street
> flash—
> blue and green and red and yellow
> looking like fireworks
> fighting hard
> to explode.

Iki should portray something smart, stylish, or chic, for example:

> I looked in the window and saw
> a baby diamond lying on a piece
> of old, soft, blue velvet.

> The bucket seats
> in my brother's new car
> were
> pillow-soft
> and
> blue-beautiful.

Jimi should portray images that are traditional, old-fashioned, or *seemingly* dull and commonplace. (While working with a group of teachers, one immediately responded with an example —"Our Board of Education!")

> The knife, fork, and spoon
> were set down on the table
> for the hundredth time
> waiting for
> the family dinner to begin.

> The birds left the ground
> and took their proper pattern
> for flying south once again.

Shibui, according to the Japanese, is the highest form of beauty. Here something dull is written about but in the context of a rich background expressing joy or contrasting brightness:

> The sky was pitch black.
> But only until the lightning bolt
> took over and tore it apart.

> The purple pansy wasn't noticed
> until it's throat turned to a bright yellow.

These creations can be dramatically illustrated in many ways. In one fourth-grade class in New York City, a teacher used the four classifications to introduce a two-month writing lesson. Each week the children were told of one classification and were encouraged to write their thoughts. After they wrote, they mounted their compositions on colored construction paper, illustrated them, and placed them on a bulletin board display.

In the lower grades, teachers can encourage a class or small groups of children to do group exercises either independently or via the experience-chart approach. In this way children can brainstorm ideas and work and rework thoughts until perfect images are created.

TRADITIONAL VERSE FORMS

Children should also be introduced to traditional verse forms such as the couplet, the quatrain, and the limerick.

THE COUPLET

The couplet is the simplest form of poetry; it consists of two lines bound together by rhyme. Couplets have been written for centuries and centuries. As early as 1683, couplets were used to teach children both the alphabet and religious morals emphasizing the sinful nature of man. Such rhymes appeared in *The New England Primer:*

> A—In Adam's fall
> We sinned all

> Z—Zaccheus he
> Did climb a tree
> His Lord to see.

Many Mother Goose rhymes appear in the couplet form:

Tommy's tears and Mary's fears
Will make them old before their years.

January brings the snow
Makes our feet and fingers glow.

Young children will especially enjoy creating couplets. They might try writing simple verses about holidays, pets, people, food—anything.

THE QUATRAIN

The quatrain form is also appealing to children; it is written in four lines and can consist of any metrical pattern of rhyme. In Harlem one fourth-grader created a poem that tells a great deal about herself, includes excellent word images, and evokes a lot of thought. The child titled her poem "My Seed":

The seed is growing deep inside
It cannot hide, it cannot hide.
It shoves and pushes, it bangs and kicks
And one day the world will know me.

Ask your children to hunt for examples of quatrains written by master poets and read them to the class. A collection of these can prompt discussion about how much can be said in just four lines. Some examples are: Langston Hughes' "Hope," a poem about loneliness; John Ciardi's "Warning," depicting the dangers of a whirlpool; or the poem that amusingly sums up the "Four Seasons," written by an anonymous poet:

Spring: showery, flowery, bowery.
Summer: hoppy, croppy, poppy.
Autumn: wheezy, sneezy, freezy.
Winter: slippy, drippy, nippy.

Limericks immediately bring to mind the poet Edward Lear, who perfected this form to amuse the grandchildren of his friend the Earl of Derby. Lear wrote many limericks such as:

> There was an Old Man with a beard,
> Who said, "It is just as I feared!—
> Two owls and a hen,
> Two larks and a wren
> Have all built their nests in my beard!"

The form consists of five lines. Lines one, two, and five must rhyme; lines three and four may or may not rhyme.

After hearing many limericks written by Lear and others, children will want to create their own. With younger children, the limerick form might be introduced via the teacher's help. You might try this: Write one line on the chalkboard, for example: *There was a man with 33 shoes.* Encourage the children to make up a list of all the words they can think of that rhyme with *shoes.* Then they can suggest a second line for the limerick, ending with one of their words. This line is also written on the chalkboard. Next, the children can think of a third line following the thought of the limerick but not ending with a rhyming word. Now they can make a second list of words rhyming with the last word in the third line and use this as a resource to finish line four. Line five can end with a rhyming word from the first list they prepared.

In 1970 the editor of "Words to the Wise," a popular column in *Junior Scholastic* magazine, invited readers to send in their limerick creations. Hundreds of limericks poured into the office daily. Limericks were written about everything—from pure nonsense to space to sibling rivalry. Here are two examples written by sixth-graders that appeared in the January 11, 1971 issue:

I think my brother's a rat
And my sister's a terrible brat.
  My mother is spice,
  My father is nice,
And there's nothing to say of my cat.
                    —Darrell Monk
                    Crestview School
                    Vista, California

A man from the planet of Mars
Came down to Earth for some jars.
  He said to the keeper,
  "Bleep, bleep blinkee peeper,"
Then, zoom, he was gone for the stars.
                    —Celia Dye
                    East View Elementary
                    Greenville, Tennessee

The limerick form gives children the opportunity to use interesting sounding words, to experiment with language and have fun in clever ways.

An excellent collection, *Laughable Limericks* (T. Y. Crowell, 1965), has been compiled by Sara and John E. Brewton. Here you will find many of Edward Lear's limericks along with others by such notables as John Ciardi, David McCord, Eve Merriam, and the late Ogden Nash. The last section of this volume, "Writing Limericks," contains fourteen rhymes by David McCord who tells children how they, too, can create. For youngsters or teachers with musical ability, there is also sheet music to two tunes that will fit most any limerick created.

A second volume, *Typewriter Town* (E. P. Dutton, 1960) by William Jay Smith, combines pictures that were made using the typewriter with his limericks. The results are very clever and will certainly challenge older girls and boys to try limericks and create concrete type-illustrations to accompany them.

PARODIES

Children can have a great deal of fun experimenting with parodies. Limericks and Mother Goose rhymes are popular forms to use to introduce parodies. Mother Goose parodies have been treated comically in several books. In *The Charles Addams Mother Goose* (Windmill Books, distributed by Harper and Row, 1967), the renowned *New Yorker* humorist whose cartoons were the basis for the television program "The Addams Family," turns a macabre eye on twenty-six nursery rhymes. The rhymes are intact, however; they are parodied by the large, devilish, full-color illustrations of Mr. Addams. Mistress Mary, *quite* contrary, not only waters her familiar silver bells and cockleshells but also tends to poisoned mushrooms; the farmer's wife still cuts off the tails of the three blind mice —but with an *electric* carving knife!

Frederick Winsor gives space-age twists to Mother Goose rhymes in his *The Space Child's Mother Goose* (Simon and Schuster, 1956). Here Solomon Grundy walks on Monday but "time machines" on Sunday!

Mother Goose has also recently been moved to city streets. In Hilde Hoffman's, *The City and Country Mother Goose* (American Heritage Press, 1969), the artist has used over a hundred color illustrations bringing Mother into tenement houses, crowded streets, traffic jams, and subway cars.

In Eve Merriam's *The Inner City Mother Goose* (Simon and Schuster, 1969; also available in paperback), Mother Goose explodes onto the urban scene. The poems are strong; they bite, sting, and underline the horrors that exist in today's cities. Poverty, police brutality, cockroaches, and crime are several of the themes. The black and white visuals by Lawrence Ratzkin add to the dynamic words. *The Inner City Mother Goose* was not written as a children's book; it is for the mature reader. Read it carefully before you decide to bring it into the classroom.

All of these contemporary versions can be used to spark creative writing. The children themselves might offer some fun ideas for parodies, too. Why not have the children set some of the Mother Goose rhymes in an amusement park, as Hollywood or television personalities, or at the seashore? One fourth-grader offered:

> Little Boy Blue, come blow your horn;
> The sheep's in the meadow, the cow's in the corn.
> Where is the boy that looks after the sheep?
> He's down at the seashore buying hot dogs cheap!

A fifth-grade child came up with:

> There was an old woman
> Who lived in a shoe
> She had so many children...
> That she looked in the Yellow Pages
> And called a Real Estate Man.

Elliot Horne has written a comical article, "A Diller, A Dollar, an A&R Scholar" (*New York Times*, December 27, 1970, p. 19), in which he sets Mother Goose rhymes in a contemporary rock music setting. Two parodies from the article include:

> As I was going along, long, long,
> A-singing a comical song, song, song,
> The lane that I went was long, long, long,
> And the song that I sung was a long, long, song,
> And so I went singing along.
> And they released it as an album.

Ride a cockhorse to Banbury Cross,
To see an old lady upon a white horse;
Rings on her fingers and bells on her toes,
She shall have music wherever she goes.
As long as her transistors hold out.

An excellent resource to have on hand when introducing parody is *Speak Roughly to Your Little Boy: A Collection of Parodies and Burlesques Together with Original Poems Chosen and Annotated for Young People* (Harcourt, 1971), edited by the poet Myra Cohn Livingston and illustrated by Joseph Low. In this spirited volume, Mrs. Livingston presents a wide array of poems followed by a parody and/or burlesque. Thus we find the cumulative nursery rhyme "The House that Jack Built" followed by G. E. Bates' "Pentagonia," a clever parody about the building of the Pentagon in Washington, D. C. The poems and parodies have been largely drawn from the work of English and American poets—Edward Lear, Edgar Allan Poe, and Lewis Carroll, but you will also find William Carlos Williams, David McCord, and Phyllis McGinley represented.

EXPERIMENTAL VERSE FORMS

Two experimental verse forms that have recently been popularized, used, enjoyed, and written by girls and boys are concrete poetry and found poetry.

CONCRETE POETRY

Concrete poems are picture poems made out of letters and words; they are strongly visual, breaking away from any and all traditional poetic forms—poetry to be seen and felt more than to be read or heard. Here is an example of a poem in concrete:

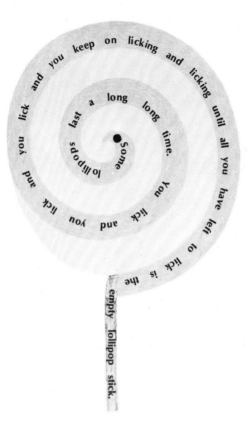

This example is taken from *The Laugh Book* (Scholastic Book Services) by Ruth Belov Gross. Three other concrete poems appear in this excellent volume for primary-grade youngsters; one is about a clock, another about rain falling, and the third is an exciting three-page poem about a ride on a roller coaster.

Two books of concrete poetry for older children to enjoy are *Poems to Hear and See* (Macmillan, 1971) by Ian Hamilton Finlay and *Street Poems* (McCall's, 1971) by Robert Froman.

In Mr. Finlay's slim volume, words are freely used to form a variety of associations, sounds, and images. In "Acrobats," for example, the eight letters of the word are arranged in a multitude of ways on the page to suggest performing acrobats. The poet lives in a small, Scottish farmhouse, in the Pentland Hills made famous by Robert Louis Stevenson. He established his own small press and prints many of his poems in book, poster, and postcard form. Some of his poems have even been constructed in wood, glass, and stone to stand in gardens.

Robert Froman's book contains fifty-six concrete poems all relating to the urban experience; these deal with pollution, traffic, skyscrapers—and one is even written in honor of a garbage truck.

FOUND POETRY

Found poems are poems that just happen to be around—words that already have been written somewhere—on menus, labels, in newspaper advertisements, or signs on streets.

Children can be encouraged to look for striking phrases or sentences, write them down, and then arrange them in a series of lines in poetic forms.

Pop Poems by Ronald Gross (Simon and Schuster, 1967), contains found poems from a variety of sources including a menu featuring prime steak, a Barbie-Doll advertisement, and government reports.

The following found poem was arranged by a fifth-grader. In an advertisement for Swank jewelry, the child found the following words: "French cuffs should be noticed, not taken for granted. Cuff links are now, cuff links are fashion, cuff links are for everyone." He arranged these words on a large piece of oak tag and titled his composition "The Link":

> French cuffs
>> should be noticed,
> Not
>> taken for granted;
> Cuff links
>> are now,
> Cuff links
>> are fashion,
> Cuff links
>> are
>>> for everyone

On the oak tag he fastened one cuff link to represent the period at the end of the last line. Around the poem he pasted pictures cut from magazines, showing people wearing cuff links.

Children can begin to look for common everyday writing that appears in media or on signs they see around their immediate neighborhoods. A third-grader found the following words in a nearby supermarket window and arranged it:

> Did you
>> cash in
>>> your Brillo
>>>> coupon
>>>>> today?
> If not,
>> why
>>> not?

Of course children are not writing poetry, but they are showing creativity and a knowledge of the ways language can be made into a visual image.

ADULTS WHO HAVE HELPED CHILDREN WRITE

In today's busy world, some educators have recognized the creative abilities children possess. This is not to say that educators in the past have not recognized and developed the creative poetic potential of children. As early as 1929, Hugh Mearns' *Creative Power: The Education of Youth in the Creative Arts* was published (available in paperback from Dover). In this classic volume, the author discusses a multitude of ways he released creativity in children. The text contains fresh imagery developed by girls and boys; "How Worms Walk," saying goodbye to worn-out shoes, and selfishness are among the themes. In the chapter "Other Rhymings," Mr. Mearns points out that forced rhyming places restrictions upon first-grade children, stifling creativity. He shows how rhyming can produce mere doggerel rather than releasing poetic imagery—the fresh spontaneous language that children are so apt to produce when set free.

More recently, several people working with children have taken a careful, serious look at children's writings. In the beginning of this chapter, Richard Lewis's *Miracles* was discussed. In Appendix II: *Outstanding Volumes of Poetry by Children for Children,* you can find much evidence of children's creative potential. Naturally, published works receive widespread attention, but there are just as many ideas and as much creativity bottled up among the girls and boys sitting in your very own class. The point is to motivate a child to write, to free his thoughts —and himself.

One highly successful program is the Teachers and Writers Collaborative. Until 1969 this group was supported by the National Endowment for the Humanities and received additional support from the New York State Council on the Arts. Presently the group is operating on a grant from the Field Foundation. The group's beliefs rest on several assumptions:

1. Children who are allowed to develop their own language naturally, without the imposition of artificial standards of grading, usage, and without arbitrary limits on subject matter, are encouraged to expand the boundaries of their own language usage;

2. Grammatical and spelling skills develop as a result of an attachment to language and literature, not vice versa. The attempt to teach skills before they are proved to have any relevance or relation to the child's interests and needs has been one of the primary causes of stifling of children's interest in language;

3. Children who write their own literature and who read the productions of other children are more likely to view all literature as an effort to deal with one's experience in creative ways, whatever that experience may consist of.

To accomplish these goals the group places professional writers who work on a regular basis with teachers interested in exposing their children to new ways of using language. The writers maintain detailed diaries of their work with teachers and students; these diaries, together with children's work, become the raw material for the project's publications—newsletters, curriculum materials, and anthologies. A subscription to the *Teachers and Writers Collaborative Newsletter* is $3.00 for four issues; it is available from Teachers and Writers Collaborative, Pratt Center for Community Improvement, 244 Vanderbilt Avenue, Brooklyn, New York 11205.

Don't let the word *Newsletter* fool you. The booklets abound with ideas that have been tried and tested throughout the elementary, junior high, and high school grades. The publication, usually eighty pages, contains drawings and exciting graphics done by children. In one issue, for example (October 1970), the table of contents listed several techniques that stimulate boys and girls to truly create:

1. Mirrors involved children's thinking about what happens when they stand in front of a big mirror, and then, like Alice, what might happen if they, themselves, could walk right through

the looking-glass. The children's responses in prose and poetry are wildly imaginative.

2. Junk is another topic from which children created responses to the stuff in their pockets, closets, and lives as well as junk in the environment.

3. Talking Jismoes encourage children to think of themselves as inanimate objects—what would they think about, feel, and say if they were a can of green beans or a fork; what dialogue would be written if a desk, chair, computer, Kellogg's breakfast foods, chow mein, and soap were talking together?

4. Poetry Charades involves the use of the body to spark the imagination.

5. Bestiary invites boys and girls to invent imaginary animals such as an *alorse,* a horse made of the alphabet.

The three dollars you'll invest in these issues will bring you hundreds of ideas from the experiences of some of the best teachers involved with children. And since each idea has been tried and samples of children's work are provided, you just cannot go wrong.

Stephen M. Joseph's *The Me Nobody Knows: Children's Voices from the Ghetto* (Avon, 1969, paperback) has enjoyed a huge success both as a book and a Broadway musical. The volume is filled with prose and poetry written by children from ages seven to eighteen, most of whom are black or Puerto Rican. There are four sections in the work: "How I See Myself," "How I See My Neighborhood," "The World Outside," and "Things I Can't See or Touch."

Recently Kenneth Koch and his book *Wishes, Lies and Dreams: Teaching Children to Write Poetry* (Chelsea House; distributed by Random House, 1971; also available in paperback) have both made headlines and served as the basis for many articles. Mr. Koch, a poet and teacher, taught writing to adults at New York's New School. In 1968, under the sponsorship of the American Academy of Poets, he began an experiment with children at P.S. 61 in Manhattan. All kinds of ideas to stimulate children to write were tested out by Mr. Koch; the results of his efforts are contained in his book.

In an article, " 'On Christmas Day No More Current Events'—Poems by Schoolchildren" (*New York Times Magazine,* December 20, 1970, pp. 5–7+), Mr. Koch commented:

When the classroom atmosphere is right, children still need some help: What should we write about? How should we do it? I give the children a poetry idea every time I go to a class. Among the best ones I found to start with are Wish Poems (begin every line with "I wish"), Comparison Poems (a comparison in every line), Noise Poems (how something sounds in every line), I Used To—But Not Now Poems (comparisons between the present and the past), Lie Poems (every line in some way untrue), Color Poems (a different color in every line).

Twenty-three examples of students' prose and poetry are included in this article; the selections are taken from his book.

In *The Storefront* (Harper and Row; also available in paperback, 1971), Ned O'Gorman describes a community of children on 129th Street and Madison Avenue, situated in the heart of Harlem. In his first chapter, Mr. O'Gorman points out the despair of the ghetto and how children's lives have become a confusion of hopelessness and grief. It is easy to cite America's inequities, but when a man comes along and does something about them, cares, helps even a handful of children realize what they are, who they are, achieve some sense of identity, there is cause for at least one loud hoo-ray! This small, important volume is not an anthology of children's writings. Several examples are included, but the book as a whole is about the children and is filled with great insight and understanding of the importance of allowing children to discover, to feel that they, too, can make contributions to the world at large—to be!

Mr. O'Gorman went to Harlem in 1966 to work as a volunteer in a summer program sponsored by the Office of Economic Opportunity. That same fall he returned to open his storefront. What he did and what he learned is described within his ninety-one important pages. *The Storefront* is a must-read book for anyone and everyone dealing with children, whether they are in Peoria, Scarsdale, Watts, or serving in a distant land as a Peace Corps volunteer.

In 1968, June Jordan and Terri Bush began a creative writing workshop in the Fort Greene section of Brooklyn, New York. At first they were sponsored by the Teachers and Writers Collaborative Program. After this they continued working with black and Puerto Rican children on a volunteer basis. The work of these children was published in a weekly magazine called *The Voice of the Children,* and finally many of the writings were published in a book of the same title (Holt; also available in paperback, 1971). This collection of prose and poetry represents the work of twenty-seven youngsters ranging in age from nine through seventeen. An exciting part of this volume, one that will have particular appeal to teachers, is the "Afterword" in which Miss Jordan discusses the project. Included are many candid photographs of the young authors.

Young Voices (New York: Bruce Publishing Co., 1971), edited by Charles E. Schaefer and Kathleen C. Miller, is a result of a city-wide search conducted among fourth-, fifth-, and sixth-grade children in the New York metropolitan area by the Creativity Center of Fordham University. Over 21,000 poems were submitted and screened by a panel of sixteen educators. The final 123 selections were written by children ages nine through twelve, are representative of the children of New York, and cover the widest possible range of ethnic, cultural, and socio-economic levels.

The anthologist Arnold Adoff also searched for poetry. His volume, *It Is the Poem Singing into Your Eyes* (New York: Harper, 1971; also available in paperback), contains poetry selected from over 6,000 manuscripts received from forty states, Canada, Denmark, Japan, and Mexico.

A noteworthy publication that includes poetry by children is *Kids,* a magazine written and illustrated by children for children. The magazine welcomes contributions from children under sixteen. Yearly subscriptions are $5.00 with discounts on quantity orders sent to one address. For further information write to *Kids* Magazine, Box 30, Cambridge, Massachusetts 02139.

Such books should be made available so that children can share the thoughts of their peers. After several years of collecting children's writings from you own classes, you will be able to draw upon and share the poetry written by former students, many of whom may be related to or be friends of the children in your current class.

Many worthy writing projects go unnoticed by the public. Classroom newspapers, for examples, contain a great deal of fine poetry written by children, much of which is as good as or better than that in print. Again, the important thing is to encourage children to write—to express a special feeling or a thought and let it rest on a piece of paper for someone else to read or hear.

Children's voices are all around us—in the cities, in the mountains of Appalachia, on Indian reservations, in small towns. No matter where they are they should—and *must*—be heard by someone. A friend or a relative perhaps may hear, but the very best person to hear the voices is you.

PUBLISHED POETS CAN INSPIRE CREATIVITY

Another good approach to encouraging children to write is having them try their hands at creating images similar to ones produced by poets. Five volumes that have proved to be successful in the elementary classroom are three books by Mary O'Neill—*Hailstones and Halibut Bones* (Doubleday, 1961), *People I'd Like to Keep* (Doubleday, 1963), and *Fingers Are Always Bringing Me News* (Doubleday, 1969)—and two by Carmen Bernos de Gatztold—*Prayers from the Ark* (Viking, 1962) and *The Creature's Choir: A Companion to Prayers from the Ark* (Viking, 1965; both available in paperback), and translated by Rumer Godden.

Hailstones and Halibut Bones, subtitled *Adventures in Color,* contains twelve poems about different colors. Each asks, a question: "What is Gold?" "What is Black?" or "What is Orange?" The poems not only tell about the color of objects but touch upon the ways color can make us feel; for example, *Orange is brave/Orange is bold; Gold is feeling/Like a king; Blue is feeling/Sad or low.*

The poems stir our senses and make us want to look around carefully to see everyday colors we have taken for granted and do something about them in poetic imagery. To further encourage children to create color images, bring to class specific objects—a rose, a bunch of colored leaves, or a black ant.

Nina Willis Walter, author of *Let Them Write Poetry* (Holt, 1962), discusses how she helped sixth-graders to think through the color green in the chapter "Adventures in Beauty." In her article "Miss Brown, Cleo, and Dandelions," (*Today's Catholic Teacher,* September 13, 1968, pp. 35–6+), she describes a second-grade class that wrote color poems after discussing a patch of dandelions in a vacant lot near the school. Children began to carefully look at the dandelions. One child remarked, "The dandelions are yellow." After some pushing from the teacher, "Yellow like what?" the child replied, "Like the sun. Like *pieces* of the sun." Another child saw the dandelions as resembling Easter eggs; another was impressed by the white tops.

These boys and girls were beginning to see color in new and fresh ways, to think, make comparisons, write, and speak with poetic imagery.

Janet Peterson of the Red Rock School in Las Vegas, Nevada, asks her children to describe their thoughts about colors that are not often written about. She asks, "How do certain colors make you feel?" Several responses from her classroom include:

Aqua makes me feel like a mermaid dancing in the sea.

Bronze makes me feel like a dead statue.

Amber makes me feel like millions of waves of grain.

People I'd Like to Keep contains fifteen poems about such people as "The Balloon Man," "Miss Hortense Rogers, the Grade School Principal," a doctor, a baker, and a shoe repairman. After hearing these selections by Mary O'Neill, girls and boys might think of people they'd like to keep—the custodian, a favorite teacher, or the local pet shop owner. Their poems might be given to favorite people as a gift.

In *Fingers Are Always Bringing Me News,* the poet describes many kinds and shapes of fingers. Boys and girls can try to create poems about their own fingers or fingers that they know. In a New Jersey classroom, a third-grade teacher correlated this book with a bulletin board display entitled *Our Fingers.* Each child traced the outline of his hand on a piece of construction paper. Their poems were printed on the outline and pasted onto the display. The following example is an unsophisticated poem but a good one considering it came from a child who had never written poetry before:

My Fingers
Five fingers on each hand
But some work more for me,
But I want all five of
my fingers
And I'll never settle
for just the best
three.

Prayers from the Ark offers twenty-seven short poems; *The Creature's Choir,* twenty-five. Each of the poems are simple prayers to God spoken by one of the animals on Noah's Ark—goldfish, mouse, goat, elephant, or ox. These books can also stimulate children to think quickly, to place themselves in the roles of various animals, and to pray for individual needs.

Dr. Nancy Larrick at Lehigh University in Bethlehem, Pennsylvania, conducted a Third Workshop in Poetry for Children during the spring of 1967. Twenty-two teachers met for three hours each Wednesday afternoon to read and experiment with effective ways of using poetry with children. The teachers' classrooms became laboratories where about 500 elementary school children listened to, read, recited, sang, and created poetry.

The teachers used both *Hailstones and Halibut Bones* and *Prayers from the Ark*. The results of the children's work were collected by Dr. Larrick in *Green Is Like a Meadow of Grass*, (Garrard Publishers, 1968)—the title stemming from a three-line image by an eight-year-old girl.

A section in the volume also entitled "Green Is Like a Meadow of Grass" contains ten poems written by girls and boys seven- to ten-years-old. In this chapter children write of the color blue as being "like the wind staggering/Through the sky," and gray, "a feeling/like forgetting your lunch." In the section "Our Prayers from the Ark," eleven poems written by children ranging in age seven to thirteen appear. After they had read de Gasztold's *Prayers,* children created their own images about such animals as "The Snake," "The Mouse," "The Giraffe," and "A Spider." Reading other children's work to your own boys and girls will encourage them to set forth their own thoughts.

In "Carmen Bernos de Gasztold's *Prayers From the Ark:* An Approach to Writing Poetry" written by Aaron Bernarr Beard (*Elementary English,* November 1968, pp. 968–71), the appeal of de Gasztold's poetry and how it works for students of junior high school age is discussed. Six poems composed by students at the Hillside Junior High School in Salt Lake City, Utah, are included.

If such a variety of children across the country can create such verse—so can yours!

FOR FURTHER READING

Carlson, Ruth Kearney. "The Sunset Is a Pretty Pink Dove—Children's Voices in Poetry," *Elementary English,* October 1969, pp. 748–57.

The author discusses various books of poetry written by children.

————. *Language Sparklers for the Intermediate Grades.* Berkeley, Calif.: Wagner Printing Company, 1968.

Chapter three, "Crystal Thoughts on Poetry," offers a host of ideas on developing skills in writing poetry.

————. *Sparkling Words: Two Hundred Practical and Creative Writing Ideas.* Berkeley, Calif.: Wagner Printing Company, 1965.

Chapter four, "Topaz Thoughts," cites ideas to spark creative, poetic writing experiences. Many examples of children's work are included.

————. *Writing Aids Through the Grades: One Hundred Eighty-Six Developmental Writing Activities.* New York: Teachers College Press, 1970.

Two chapters deal with writing poetry: "Oriental Poetry and other Syllabic Verse Forms" (for the intermediate grades) and "Traditional and Experimental Verse Forms."

Flood, Sister Maria Winifred. "The Wonder of Life in the Magic of Words." *Elementary English,* April, 1972, pp. 587–90.

Reading, writing and getting first-grade children to truly love poetry is the subject of this article.

Goba, Ronald J. "Poetry and the Senses," *The Clearing House,* November 1969, pp. 149–51.

The author, an assistant professor of English at Westfield State College in Westfield, Massachusetts, discusses how he gets students to write poetry based on "The Five Senses of Man." He shows one student's efforts after turning him loose—to go outside and record sensory perceptions—and how this experience led to the creation of a poem. Although the article describes work done with high school students, the information can be applied to any grade level.

Hopkins, Lee Bennett. "Breaking the Verse Barrier," *Catholic School Journal,* October 1967, pp. 52–3.

Haiku, cinquain, and sijo are discussed; samples of children's writings are included.

————. "For Creative Fun, Let Them Try a Cinquain," *Grade Teacher,* December 1966, pp. 83, 108.

Two forms of the cinquain verse form are presented along with samples of children's work from Fair Lawn, New Jersey, and Harlem, New York.

————. "From 'Trudeau's Garden," *Elementary English,* October 1967, pp. 613–4. (Reprint entitled *Breaking the Verse Barrier* available from Bank Street College Book Store, 610 West 112th St., New York, N.Y. 10025, for 25¢).

A detailed biographical account of the life of Adelaide Crapsey, the originator of the cinquain verse form. Work from the poet's book, *Verse,* is cited, along with examples of children's work in urban and suburban areas. A poem, "Adelaide Crapsey" by Carl Sandburg, is included.

————, and Misha Arenstein. "Harlem Songs with Strange Sounding Names: Cinquain, Haiku, Senryu, and Sijo," in *Classroom Practices in Teaching English: A Seventh Report of the NCTE Committee on Classroom Practices.* Champaign, Ill.: National Council of Teachers of English, 1969, pp. 34–7.

The authors detail means by which youngsters with weak backgrounds in written expression can be spurred to write short, structured verse. The article contains examples of student work done at the fifth-grade level.

Musso, Barbara Banner. "Want to Stimulate Poetry? Try This," *Grade Teacher,* November 1966, p. 86.

The author presents examples of third-graders' and one fifth-grader's work in the area of the four classifications of beauty defined by the Japanese.

Nichols, Norma S. "Poetry in the Second Grade," *Grade Teacher,* September 1969, pp. 176–82.

A discussion on how poems by John Ciardi, William Butler Yeats, and Vachel Lindsay have been used to stimulate second graders to write their own poetry.

Now Poetry. Columbus, Ohio: American Education Publications.

In this 64-page English unit book, a wide variety of poems and poetic forms are included to motivate youngsters to write. Although the booklet is geared to junior high school students, most of the forms can be used with children in the upper-elementary grades.

"Pep Up Their Verse Writing with a Poetry Booklet," *Grade Teacher,* November 1965, pp. 66–7, 142+.

Four approaches to the poem-booklet idea are discussed.

Rodgers, Dennis. "A Process for Poetry Writing," *Elementary School Journal,* March 1972, pp. 294–303.

The author identifies objectives, cites how he attained them, and tells how he moved his children from poetic form to content. Ideas and samples of children's writings are included.

Smith, Elaine Campbell. "Simile, Darn You, Simile." *Elementary English,* April, 1972, pp. 585–86.

The author gets her point across about the value of similes in an outrageously clever simile-laden article.

Stein, Debra. "Thousands of Classroom Poets," *Today's Education,* February 1972, pp. 18–20.

Mrs. Stein, Coordinator of Creative Writing for the New Jersey State Council on the Arts, reports on the various ways poets-in-residence have sparked children to write poetry.

Walter, Nina Willis, *Let Them Write Poetry.* New York: Holt, 1962 (also available in paperback).

A handbook about teaching poetry appreciation through the writing of poetry. Hundreds of examples of children's writings appear.

Weiger, Myra. "Found Poetry," *Elementary English,* December, 1971, pp. 1002–4.

A discussion of found poetry is presented along with fifteen examples found in such books as *Charlotte's Web* by E. B. White and *The Wind in the Willows* by Kenneth Grahame and in various magazine articles.

Wolsch, Robert A., *Poetic Composition Through the Grades.* New York: Teachers College Press, 1970.

Dr. Wolsch writes of the nature and worth of poetic composition and shows through anecdotes how teachers help children find their individual powers of expression. The text is filled with valuable, workable ideas.

Illustration by Irene Haas from *Something Special* © 1958, by Beatrice Schenk de Regniers. Reprinted by permission of Harcourt Brace Jovanovich, Inc.

"THE WATER'S STARTING TO BLEED!"

A POTPOURRI OF POETRY IDEAS

In this chapter dozens of ideas for motivating and following-up poetry programs throughout the grades are suggested. No attempt has been made to assign grade levels to these projects; all of them can, and have been, effectively used or adapted to fit any grade level. A variety of themes are presented to tie-in with most areas of the curriculum. None of the projects involve excessive time or unusual materials. Items like shoeboxes, string, and styrofoam can be more valuable than expensive, commercial kits of materials you can buy. With a little bit of imagination, and an occasional trip to F. W. Woolworth's, you will find that your students will be passing the poetry all year long with pride and pleasure.

The chapter begins with ideas for using Mother Goose throughout the grades, followed by ideas presented in alphabetical order of project titles.

MOTHER GOOSE GROWS AND GROWS

Mother Goose rhymes serve as an excellent introduction to poetry as well as being an important part of our literary heritage. Boys and girls of all ages can have a great time with the melodies, rhythm, and language and will find that the Mother of us all can provide innumerable opportunities for many imaginative and creative activities.

107

Recently a first-grade class in Harlem produced "Mother Goose Comes to New York," in which they created their own parodies based on the popular rhymes. A third-grade class in Virginia had a "Mother Goose Festival"; a sixth-grade class in New Jersey produced an extraordinary "Mother Goose Pageant" which the entire school enjoyed in the assembly.

MOTHER GOOSE VILLAGE

After the children are familiar with a variety of Mother Goose collections, begin planning the Village. The children can be asked which rhymes they would like to dramatize and what costumes, props, and scenery will be needed. Once the projects have been chosen, the Village can be mapped out. Street signs such as Jack Horner's Corner or King Cole's Court can be made by the children and placed around the room to show the location of the various projects.

The entrance to your classroom can become a giant shoe. Let the children help decide what to measure to find out how large the shoe should be. Sketch an outline of the shoe and the doorway on a large piece of brown wrapping paper for children to paint and cut out. After the shoe is framed around the doorway, it can be decorated with photographs of the children —the inhabitants and stars of the Mother Goose Village. A sign that says "Welcome to Mother Goose Village" might provide a final touch.

For Mary Mary's Garden children's paper flower creations can be attached to sticks and planted in styrofoam-filled shoeboxes, which can then be set "all in a row" and covered with green crepe paper borders. The garden can also become a birthday garden by having the girls and boys draw daisies with brightly colored petals on plain white paper plates. The eye of each daisy can contain a child's name and birthdate. Each daisy can be attached to a stick or colored straw and planted.

A large, rectangular cardboard box can easily serve as Humpty Dumpty's wall. Children can draw or paint bricks on the box, and Humpty can be fashioned from a large balloon. Paint on facial features with a felt-tip pen. Use cellophane tape to add a hat and a paper necktie and then tape Humpty to the wall to await his fate. When the moment for the great fall comes, a child can pierce the balloon with a pin. Be sure that you have an extra balloon on hand as an understudy just in case Humpty explodes before his cue!

A cockhorse for the Lady of Banbury Cross can be made from a broom. A paperbag horse face can cover the straw. Rags, crepe paper, or colored yarns can be tied around the end of the stick to make a tail.

What rhymes take place in the country? What rhymes take place in the city? Two backdrops can be planned to provide extra space for performers. A "rural mural" can include a haystack for Little Boy Blue, a meadow, a barn for the cow, and so on. A "city mural" might include some of the shops mentioned in the rhymes.

CREATIVE DRAMATICS TECHNIQUES

There are many ways to dramatize Mother Goose rhymes. Some can be recited by one child or a chorus; others can be sung by children using traditional music or their own melodies. The abilities of the children and the rhymes themselves will dictate the most appropriate form.

Short familiar rhymes such as "Jack and Jill," "Little Jack Horner," and "Little Miss Muffet" are easy to act out without words. The audience can guess the name of the rhyme depicted in the pantomime.

Longer narrative rhymes such as "Old Mother Hubbard"

or rhymes that can be expanded such as "Tom, Tom, the Piper's Son" are best enacted with puppets. For "Old Mother Hubbard," one child might narrate while others recreate the action and improvise dialogue for the puppet characters. For "Tom, Tom, the Piper's Son," children can be encouraged to supply a motive for Tom's crime. Questions such as: Why did Tom steal the pig? Who was his father? What do pipers do? or Was Tom rich or poor? can get things rolling.

Involve one group of children in a "Countdown for a Cow." The cow is leaving for the moon. Present at the countdown are the cat and the fiddle, the dish and spoon, and other animals and objects invented by the children, who can dress up in paperbag masks. One child can act as a news reporter and ask such questions as: Why is the cow going to the moon? What are the reactions of the citizens of Mother Goose Village? Will the cow make it? Live interviews can also be successful with "Humpty Dumpty" and "The Queen of Hearts" as well as many other rhymes.

LANGUAGE GROWTH AND CRITICAL THINKING

Mother Goose is full of lost or missing things—lost sheep, lost mittens, lost mouse tails. There are also many things that could be missing—Jack Horner's plum or Miss Muffet's spider for instance. Children can draw missing objects or write the words for them on a piece of paper. The papers can then be placed into a coffee can or a cardboard well made from a carton. A child can fish out a slip of paper from the well and if he can match the object with the Mother Goose character who lost it, he can keep the paper. Advanced children may prefer writing lost and found ads, for example: "Lost—24 blackbirds. Last seen in the King's backyard."

Many foods are mentioned in the rhymes. A classroom

Mother Goose market could advertise and sell curds and whey, hot cross buns, and pease porridge hot and cold—with reduced prices for "the nine-day-old variety!" Children can make up signs listing the items and prices as well as for things out-of-stock such as "Sorry. No Bones!"

What are some jobs mentioned in the rhymes? Do any exist today? What are they called? In a job hunting game boys and girls can apply for jobs as cobblers or piemen to a modern employment agency. Can jobs be found to match their skills?

Little Miss Mouse sat on a ———? Children can make up their own rhyming words to complete lines for phonics reinforcement. Some children may be able to create Mother Goose-type rhymes about their favorite television or cartoon characters.

CULMINATING ACTIVITIES

A Pat-a-Cake Party can be planned when the show is over. Children can help bake cakes and put alphabet letters on the frosting or decorate store-bought cup cakes to serve at the party.

A picture map can be assembled from drawings made by the girls and boys of the various areas of Mother Goose Village. The finished map can be placed on a dittoed program sheet and distributed to visitors as a memento of the Village. Map skills can be reinforced by asking questions: How can we get from one area of the Village to another? What places do we have to pass? What is the best route?

POETRY ACTIVITIES FOR ALL GRADES

In addition to Mother Goose, try the following activities to involve children in all kinds of poetry.

111

BEST POEM OF THE MONTH

At the beginning of each month, encourage children to find poems characteristic of that month. In February, for example, children might find poems entitled "February" or discover poems about Lincoln's Birthday, Valentine's Day, George Washington's Birthday, or a poem by a black poet to commemorate Negro History Week. Time can be set aside each week for children to read aloud the poems they have found and to tell why they chose them. The poems can be written out and tacked onto a bulletin board or hanging display.

During the last week of the month, the class can vote on The Best Poem of the Month and select several runners-up. The winners can be kept in a shoebox poetry file that can serve as a good place for children to find favorite poems to read again and again. The file can also be used from year to year; this is as an excellent resource for future classes.

In a Texas classroom, one teacher used this idea and correlated it with a Hanging Calendar—a clothesline stretched across the back of the room. When the children brought in poems relating to special events—holidays, children's birthdays, local events—they were placed upon the line and labeled with specific dates. General poems about the month, such as seasonal pieces, were also attached to the line.

Another teacher who used this technique held a Poetry Festival at the end of each month. Each of the poems selected by the class were once again read aloud—but this time to another class. Children practiced their selections, several acted them out, others used simple props for their poetry reading, and some did projects to accompany the poems.

Wherever this idea is tried, the unexpected happens. In one class, six children had April birthdays. During that month many boys and girls brought in birthday poems. The best poem in the opinion of that classroom was Rose Fyleman's "The Birthday Child" (in *Round the Mulberry Bush,* Dodd, Mead, 1955).

In another classroom, during December, with the hustle and bustle of the holiday season, a first snowfall, two birthdays, several miscellaneous events, *and* the acquisition of a pet hamster—guess what poem was selected as the best poem? One youngster found Marci Ridlon's delightful "Hamsters" (in *That Was Summer,* Follett, 1969) to surprise and delight both members of the class and the teacher.

BOO POEMS TO BE SCARED BY

Halloween is one of the favorite holidays on the school calendar. Children can be "well-scared" by reading poems about ghosts and goblins, witches and wizards, and other eerie creatures and characters that make appearances during the Halloween season. To add spice to the holiday, children can create their very own witches. Peel an apple for each child and allow them to sculpt it to resemble a witch's head. Black construction paper can be used for her hat and gown. Whole cloves can serve as eyes and blackened teeth. Within several days the apples will naturally shrivel and discolor, giving the witch an even spookier look. Children can take the apples home to put in their windows or use as table displays on Halloween.

Two excellent sources of boo poems are *Shrieks at Midnight: Macabre Poems, Eerie and Humorous* (T. Y. Crowell, 1969) selected by Sara and John E. Brewton, and *The Haunted House and Other Spooky Poems and Tales* (Scholastic Book Services, 1970), edited by Vic Crume and Gladys Schwarcz.

Shrieks at Midnight contains poems about restless spirits roaming the earth and modern ghosts who were done-in for daring to fold up an IBM card. There are poems by Lewis Carroll, John Ciardi, and Langston Hughes to truly scare the pants off your students.

The Haunted House and Other Spooky Poems and Tales is a paperback containing thirty-five poems and stories on ghostly or mysterious themes, including the poems "Winter Moon" by Langston Hughes, "The Bat" by Theodore Roethke, the limerick "A Young Lady from Glitch" by Tamara Kitt, and the extraordinarily frightening tale "The Velvet Ribbon" by Ann McGovern. There is also a book-record combination in which the 7-inch, LP recording contains selections from the book performed by Paul Hecht and Carole Danell. Play the record on Halloween Day with the lights turned out and a candle flickering on your desk. It will surely produce delightful shivers for your very own witches and goblins.

BOXES AND POETRY

The six sides of a small cardboard box provide ample opportunity for displaying children's interpretations of favorite poems. Secure the cover on the box with tape. Children can paint upon the surface or decorate the box with cloth or paper.

After they have selected a poem, they can mount illustrative material on all six sides of the box. This technique can be used on any grade level. One sixth-grade student brought in a commercial photo cube, an inexpensive plastic cube available in most novelty stores. He used a Polaroid camera to shoot photographs of New York harbor. The finished pictures were placed in the photo cube to dramatically depict Langston Hughes' "Waterfront Streets" (in Langston Hughes' *Selected Poems,* Alfred A. Knopf, 1966).

Shoeboxes were used by a second-grade teacher to enrich a unit on the zoo. Her children used these to represent animal cages. The insides of the shoeboxes were painted. Interesting papers provided collage landscapes. Finally, animal drawings were put into the shoeboxes. Bars, for the most ferocious animals, were made from strips of paper and yarn and glued over the sides of the box. Several of the children's works were very humorous. Henry's giraffe, for example, projected through a slit in the top of the shoebox, insuring room for Mr. Giraffe's very large, spotted neck; Edith's elephant's trunk was far too long for a shoebox cage, thus, it protruded through the side of the box; Roy's lion's tail stuck out through a slit in the side of the box where a tiny paper mouse rested.

Poems about the various animals were found and placed alongside the children's artwork.

BUILDING POEMS

A New Jersey teacher tied poetry and art together in a unit on community planning and construction. The poems included Eve Merriam's "Bam, Bam" (in *Catch a Little Rhyme,* Atheneum, 1966) and Myra Cohn Livingston's, "Construction" (in *A Crazy Flight and Other Poems,* Harcourt, 1969).

The teacher encouraged the children to bring to class a variety of materials gathered at a nearby building site. Bricks, scraps of wood, nails, and plaster were used by the class to construct sculptures and collages. Finished projects were put together in a hall display.

COLLAGE POETRY BALLS

After each child has selected a favorite poem, encourage him to create a collage poetry ball. Children's collages interpreting the poem can be placed on large circles cut from oak tag. Photographs from newspapers or magazines, cloth, realia, various sizes of print or type, and original drawings can be the raw material to depict the poem's meaning.

Shirley McCammon, an English teacher, used a variation of this idea to encourage her students to write their own poetry. In an article, "From Collages to Poetry" (in *Humanizing English: Do Not Fold Spindle or Mutilate: An Eighth Report of the Committee on Classroom Practices, 1970–1971,* edited by Edward R. Fagan and Jean Vandell, pp. 19–22; available from National Council of Teachers of English), the author describes her classes' work in collage; these were entitled "I Am" and motivated the child to ask himself, "Who am I? Where am I going? Where did I come from?" After the collages were completed, each student wrote several sentences about himself. This led to the creation of poems after each student had worked and reworked his original lists. One example follows:

List of Sentences:
I am inhibited to degrees
Filled with mixed emotions.
Unhappy at times, full of life.
Lonely and popular.
I am one and the same.
I am unique.
I am ME!

The Poem:
Inhibited, filled with emotions,
Unhappy at times,
Though full of life.
Lonely, yet popular,
I am uniquely ME.

Although this project was carried out with high school students, the same technique can be used with children on any grade level, particularly boys and girls in the middle grades. Children can create collages focusing around their homes, families, special interests and hobbies, pets, peers, or aspirations; they can then try to write a poem about themselves and their collage constructions.

Collages can also be turned into poetry wall hangings. Children can mount wallpaper onto large, rectangular pieces of cardboard and then illustrate their interpretation of poems with collage materials. The panels can be used for hall or classroom bulletin board displays and later taken home by youngsters to hang in their own homes.

COLOR ME POETRY

Several ways to involve children with finding or writing poems about color have been successful. One teacher placed a bright array of colored wrapping tissue on a bulletin board with the caption, "Find a Poem About Me."

A dramatic technique to stimulate children to think about color is to use an overhead projector. Place a clear bowl of water atop the projector—a plastic turtle dish or pie plate is best. By dropping a few drops of food coloring into the bowl, magical things will happen on the screen. The coloring can be stirred around or blown to create movement, or colors can be mixed together to make new color combinations.

In a kindergarten class where this was done, one small lad remarked as the color red hit the water, "Oh my God. The water's starting to bleed!"

The movement of the color can be enhanced by playing a musical selection or can be combined with dance and rhythm movements.

Paint blots are another technique that works well, particularly with older girls and boys. Children can drop a few blobs of tempera paint on construction paper and carefully fold the paper in half. When it is opened, they will find an interesting paint blob, á la Rorschach. Within the next few days they can give a title to their creation and look for appropriate poems that best illustrate their blots. The results will be surprising.

DO TELL THE SCARECROW!

A third-grade teacher in Kansas combined the book *Don't Tell the Scarecrow and Other Japanese Poems* (Four Winds Press, 1969; also available in paperback from Scholastic Book Services) with an exciting display. Children in her class had a great time building a life-sized scarecrow. Old clothes donated by fathers were stuffed with newspapers and fastened together with florist's wire. When Mr. Scarecrow was finished, he was a most impressive sight. He was dressed in shoes, pants, shirt, and coat, and his old basketball head was topped with a sailor's cap and sun glasses. All year long poems were pinned on the scarecrow. When the children wanted to read a favorite poem, they could easily go over and unpin one. A small rug, placed at his feet, made a convenient poetry reading-resting place where children could browse through poetry books.

GROWING WITH POETRY

One primary-grade teacher in Wichita, Kansas, uses a chart titled "I Have Finished Being Small" in her classroom. Inches are marked off on the chart, and there is space alongside the numbers to record children's names. Once a month, each child is measured to record his growth. The chart contains a variety of pictures and poems to be read to or by boys and girls while their heights are being recorded. Poems can include Aileen Fisher's "Growing" (in *In One Door and Out the Other*, T. Y. Crowell, 1969) or Dorothy Aldis' "Big" (in *All Together*, G. P. Putnam, 1952).

A LINE OF POETRY

Sadie Surel, a teacher in New York City, devised a good way to prompt children to search for poems. She strung a clothesline across her classroom and attached a series of brown manila envelopes to it with clothespins. Pictures were pasted on the face of each envelope—a picture of a boy, a girl, or an animal or a photograph depicting a particular season. Class members were encouraged to look for or write poems about the illustrations on the envelopes. A poetry clothesline can become a permanent fixture in the classroom and can be changed as often as needed to tie in with specific lessons.

A PEEP HOLE POETRY DISPLAY

Older boys and girls can let their imaginations run wild when creating peep hole poetry displays. Children can work individually or in groups. After a poem has been selected, the children punch a hole about the size of a pencil in one end of a shoebox; the other end is completely cut out and covered with cellophane paper. The child constructs a diorama inside the box interpreting his selected poem. When the display is completed, the boxtop is put on and a flashlight is projected through the cellophane. As one child reads the poem or hears it read on a commercial or class-made record or tape, another can peep through the hole and view the diorama.

119

Diane Weissberger, a teacher in Germantown High School, Germantown, Pennsylvania, tried a novel approach to excite students over poetry—sending them on a poetry hunt. Each student selected a theme and found ten poems related to it; these were transcribed into a huge booklet and illustrated with appropriate pictures. At the end of each book, the student wrote a concluding paragraph explaining why he chose his particular theme and how he felt about it while working on the project. She reports: "The summary paragraphs proved to me that students gained much insight into themselves and actually found poetry fun!"

This idea is one that can be used on any grade level. The number of poems selected can depend on the child's age level. Third-graders, for example, might choose three or four poems relating to a specific topic.

The basic objective is to get children to think through the *whys* of the project. Why they chose the theme they did? What sources did they draw from? What relationships did they see between the selections? How did they benefit from this project? Choosing poems helps children focus their attention on what they are reading and looking for; the child becomes a discriminating selector.

Illustrations can be original drawings or pictures collected from a variety of sources. Artwork for booklets might also be created by other students, older boys and girls, or even a child's immediate family. Finished booklets can include an attractive cover containing a good title for the work and the name of the compiler and the artist. A table of contents can be included as well as an index of titles, first lines, and poets. To add to this project, older children might include a brief biographical sketch of each poet. The last page can contain a photograph of the compiler along with a composition explaining the work.

For very young girls and boys, mimeographed poems can be provided, plus blank pages for original drawings. Mother Goose rhymes are perfect for such a booklet. Imaginations can be stretched to put Mother Goose into some of the various surroundings mentioned earlier.

A PICTURE FOR A POEM

Dig into your own personal picture file and post an interesting photograph or picture on a small bulletin board. Students can hunt for poems they feel fit the mood or describe the illustration. Catchy titles add to such displays. For example, the caption "Sneak into this haunted house" under an illustration of an old house—the "hauntier" the better—might either elicit original poems or poems such as "The House at the Corner" by Myra Cohn Livingston (in *Wide Awake and Other Poems,* Harcourt, 1959) or Joyce Kilmer's "The House with Nobody in It" (in *Silver Pennies* compiled by Blanche Jennings Thompson, Macmillan, 1925).

Other pictures and captions might deal with nature, the environment, space, sports, or the sea.

A POCKETFUL OF POEMS

Cut out several large pocket shapes from medium weight cardboard or oak tag. These pockets can be painted with tempera or covered with fabric patterns. Label each pocket with a category such as Me, The City, Insects, or Animals. Leaving the tops open, secure the pockets to a bulletin board by stapling around the edges. Insert several poems in each pocket and encourage the children to pick out and read a poem whenever they have some free classroom time. Near the bulletin board place a copy of Beatrice Schenk de Regniers' "Keep A Poem in Your Pocket" (in her book *Something Special,* Harcourt, 1958; the poem is also reprinted on page 177).

Children can be encouraged not only to pick the pockets but fill them once in awhile too!

A POEM FOR A PICTURE

Children are often asked to illustrate a poem they have read or heard. You might try turning this idea around by encouraging girls and boys to draw or paint a picture first and then find a poem that goes with it. Several children can look for poems they feel appropriate for a classmate's drawing. If they cannot find a suitable poem, they may decide to write their own. In any case, the children have looked at a variety of poems, and the next time they paint they may remember just the right verse to accompany their pictures.

POEMS TO SATISFY YOUNG APPETITES

A bulletin board can feature the question, "What's for Lunch Poems?" A table setting can be depicted by stapling a paper tablecloth on the bulletin board for a background along with paper plates, cups, and plastic cutlery. The latter can be mounted with double-faced masking tape or strong glue.

On each plate a food poem can appear. One might describe eating an ice cream cone on a summer day; another might mention the spicey taste of chili con carne or relishes on a hot dog. Before lunch hour, either a child or the teacher can read a selection from a plate.

An excellent resource for food poems is *How to Eat a Poem and Other Morsels* (Pantheon, 1967), an anthology selected by Rose Agree. The poems can be changed as regularly as the children's appetites.

POEMS TO CELEBRATE

Events in children's personal lives can encourage the sharing of poetry. Birthdays, a new baby coming into the family, or holiday celebrations can be enhanced when girls and boys design their own greeting cards. Appropriate poems can be selected or written, illustrated, and sent to individuals celebrating extra special occasions such as Mothers' Day or Fathers' Day, Valentine's Day and Christmas, of course, are ideal times to write and illustrate greeting card verses for special friends and relatives.

POET OF THE MONTH

Introducing a poet and his works can be stimulating for children in the upper-grades. Use a bulletin board and table display to highlight the poet of the month. The bulletin board can feature biographical information along with several of the poet's work printed on oak tag. If possible, a photograph of the poet should be included. A table display can feature volumes of the poet's work and, if available, a recording of his voice or readings from his works.

Often such a display sparks children to do research on the lives of other poets. Boys and girls can write letters to publishers requesting additional information, write letters to poets themselves (children's letters can be sent in care of the publishing house and will be forwarded to the poet by the editor), or look for information in books and periodicals.

A POETREE

Branches can be arranged to create a PoeTree. The branches can be attached to a wall, hung from the ceiling like a mobile, or placed in a pail or flowerpot filled with sand, earth, or styrofoam. Spray paint can change the color of the branches from time to time.

As children select and illustrate favorite poems, they can be attached to the branches for others to read. Occasionally, the PoeTree can tie in with specific curriculum learnings or have a theme assigned to it.

A New York City teacher combines this idea with Poet of the Month. Atop the tree the poet's name is printed on oak tag; when available, a picture of the poet is added. The branches of the tree are then filled with poems by the poet being honored.

The PoeTree can also be a seasonal tree. At Christmastime, for example, Christmas or winter poems might appear; in February, the PoeTree can help celebrate Negro History Week by featuring poems by or about famous blacks.

In New Jersey, a fourth-grade teacher let each child create a mini-PoeTree as gifts for Mothers' Day. Each child decorated a cardboard milk carton, filled it with earth, and then placed a small twig firmly inside. A poem or two was attached to the twig. At the top of the branch some children placed pictures of their mothers. The mini-PoeTrees were unique, unusual, inexpensive, and very effective presents.

A POETRY ANIMAL FAIR

Use a corner of the room to set up a poetry animal fair. Hang a mobile from the ceiling featuring pictures of animals. Place a large wooden box under the mobile to hold books of poems about animals together with models of animals that children find and bring into class.

After boys and girls have read many poems about animals, have them select a favorite. Drawn or cut-out pictures of animals can be pasted to cardboard and attached to sticks to make puppets. Children can work the puppets while reading their favorite poem about the animal of their choice.

A similar idea was carried out by a first-grade teacher in California. She used the theme "Fish for a Poem" and featured a fish mobile. She placed several volumes of poetry containing poems about fish and a bowl with two goldfish on a box. A second box was gaily decorated and contained poems mounted on cardboard about fish and the sea. A small hole was punched in each piece of cardboard, through which a paper clip was slipped. Children could take their "fishing poles" (long sticks with a magnet attached to the end) and literally fish for poetry.

POETRY FACE TO FACE

An inexpensive mirror can help introduce a variety of poems. The mirror can be attached to a bulletin board or hung on a wall; around it attach several poems about one's face or oneself. Near the mirror place several volumes of poetry. Poems might include "Mirror! Mirror!" by Deborah Ensign (in Richard Lewis's *Miracles,* Simon and Schuster, 1966), "Robert, Who Is Often a Stranger to Himself" by Gwendolyn Brooks (in *Bronzeville Boys and Girls,* Harper and Row, 1956), Carl Sandburg's "Phizzog" (in *Good Morning, America,* Harcourt, 1928, 1956), or Lee Bennett Hopkins, "Mirror" (in *Charlie's World,* Bobbs-Merrill, 1972).

The display might also contain pictures of the children in the class or baby pictures for peers to guess who *was* who!

POETRY HAPPENINGS

A group of children can plan poetry happenings or dramatic readings of several poems relating to a specific subject. Poems can tie in with curriculum learnings or interests on any grade level—science, social studies, mathematics, sports, or hobbies —or the group can choose the subject—rocks, the city, famous people, or music. When they have a final selection, they can present a poetry happening for the class and for other classes in the school. To enhance the happening, simple props or creative dramatics can be employed.

A POETRY JAR

June Luna, an elementary teacher in Las Vegas, Nevada, uses a clever device to motivate poetry. A clear glass jar becomes a Poetry Jar. At the beginning of each week an object is placed in the jar. Children then become poem hunters, seeking poetry that mentions or describes the object.

Objects might be toy models of cars or animals, realia such as a leaf, a rock, or a flower, or sometimes a live specimen such as an ant or a guppy. A larger container such as a fish tank might feature turtles, horntoad frogs, or interesting fish.

Alongside the jar or tank leave a pencil and a pad of paper for those who want to sit, observe, and create poetry. Girls and boys might also try creating a variety of short verse forms based on the object in the poetry jar.

POETRY PRESENTS

Teachers and students alike are always searching for the right present to give one another at Christmas or for birthdays.

Marily O'Brien and Marion Chapman, two primary-grade teachers in Las Vegas, Nevada, devised a solution. At Christmastime a tree is adorned with children's handmade decorations. Underneath the Christmas tree, each child places a poem, wrapped-up and ready to be chosen by a classmate on the last day of school prior to the holiday. On top of the tree a huge Santa Claus stands holding a seasonal poem.

The same idea can be used for classroom birthdays. As birthdays come up, children can select a poetry present from a decorated cardboard box.

A POETRY WEATHER CALENDAR

Very young boys and girls will enjoy a poetry weather calendar. Use a large piece of oak tag for each month. List the month, weeks, and days of the week, along with the question, "What is the weather like today?"

On the bottom of the chart, attach several large, brown envelopes labeled Sun Poems, Wind Poems, Cloud Poems, Rain Poems, or Snow Poems. Collected poems can be placed within the appropriate envelopes. The envelopes can be added to and used year after year. When the month, day, and date of the week have been discussed, a child can volunteer to tell what the weather is like and then choose an appropriate poem from an envelope to read or have read to the class. Weather combinations, such as sunny and windy, can also be used.

Girls and boys can be encouraged to add to the envelopes as they find various weather poems throughout the year.

Excellent resources to use along with this idea is Maurice Sendak's *Chicken Soup with Rice: A Book of Months* (Harper and Row, 1962; also available in paperback from Scholastic Book Services), and the *Chicken Soup with Rice Calendar* (Scholastic Book Services). In the book Mr. Sendak, the ac-

127

claimed author/illustrator, turns poet and sings the praises of his favorite soup in gay rhymes and pictures for each month of the year. The *Chicken Soup with Rice Calendar* has three-color illustrations and features poems for each of the twelve months; this 29½ inch x 22½ inch poster is $1.

SEE THE SEA IN POETRY

Jean C. Ronan, an elementary teacher in Las Vegas, Nevada, uses a table top display entitled "Our Home—The Sea" to tie poetry into science, art, and literature. She covers a table with sand, a variety of seashells, and starfish. The display also contains a toy shovel and pail, which serves as a container for sea poems the children in the class find or write. Behind the display she places art prints of great seascape paintings to further motivate youngsters to look at, feel, and write their own thoughts about the sea.

Several books about seashore life are also displayed to spark creative writing. All of the children's creations are placed in the pail. At the end of a given time both the poems the children found and the ones they themselves have created are bound into a huge scrapbook and illustrated with original drawings or pictures clipped from magazines and newspapers.

THE SENSES AND POETRY

Children of all ages can be sparked to create poems after they have had a variety of planned sensory experiences. One way to motivate boys and girls to use their senses is to take them for several walks around the neighborhood. Be specific on each walk. Tell the class, "Today we are going on a *hearing* walk to record only the various sounds we hear." On a second walk, children can record all that they see; or on a third, all that they smell, and so on. During each walk the class can record all the various sounds they hear, sights they see, and so forth in a notebook.

After several of these walking trips, plans can be made for a sensory field trip. Visit an area the children have never seen before; a trip to a museum or a bakery, or even a ride on a train or merry-go-round can produce excellent writings when boys and girls are offered the opportunity to open up their senses.

In *Writing Aids through the Grades* (Teachers College Press, 1970), Dr. Ruth Kearney Carlson describes such a walk—a feeling walk. One class went out and brought back such objects as twigs, clods of dirt, and leaves. These were arranged on a table with a sign that read "The Things We Touch." In her book *Sparkling Words: Two Hundred Practical and Creative Writing Ideas,* (Wagner Printing Company, 1965), the same author offers a variety of "Imagination Walks and Unusual Experiences as a Basis for Creativity" (pp. 81–8).

Several years ago, while working with Pearl Rabin, a resource teacher in Fair Lawn, New Jersey, we took a second-grade class to a pond for a seeing walk. The children saw many things but were fascinated by the many seed pods that appeared on the bank. After bringing the pods (and the children) back into the classroom, several boys and girls wrote the following:

Seed pods when they break look like bombs exploding.
Seed pods sail like parachutes when they open.
The pods look like cotton candy when they are put together.
I could eat it, but I won't.

In a section "The Creative Arts" in *Grade Teacher* (April 1966, p. 73+), Gloria Ann Morton-Finney, a third-grade teacher at George Washington Carver School in Indianapolis, told how she trains her classes to listen to nature by providing them with imaginative questions. She asks:

How does a brook sound?
What song does a cricket sing?
What tool do you think of when you hear a woodpecker?
How do raindrops sound against your umbrella?
You are on a buffalo hunt with Indian friends. What sounds do you hear as the herd draws near?

Questions such as these are excellent ones to ask before taking the class on a walking trip.

Sounds can arouse young writers. Another idea to inspire writing is to record or have children record a variety of sounds —bacon frying, the ticking of a clock, a slamming door, a baby crying, or a typewriter in action. After discussing sounds and noises and actually hearing them, a fourth-grade class in Harlem composed the following:

Noise

Noise, noise everywhere.
What to do! It's always there.
Bang! Pow! Zoom! Crunch!
Buzz! Crack! Crack! Munch!

In the air, on the ground,
Noise, noise all around.
Dogs barking, cars parking,
Planes flying, babies crying.

Sh...sh...time for sleep
Not a single little peep.
Oh no—through the door—
Comes a noisy, awful snore.

Tick-tock—stop the clock.
Stop the yelling on my block
Close the windows, shut them tight
Cotton in ear ... nighty-night

Suzanne Hunsucker, a teacher at the Riverton (Wyoming) High School, offers this idea for "sensational writing" ("Teaching Tips," *Scholastic Teacher,* senior edition, December 1970, p. 23):

... I bombarded (the children's) senses as they walked into the classroom. Beatle music was playing, crepe paper hanging. I passed out chocolate kisses and small pieces of material to feel, and I sprayed the air with spice room deodorizer. All this launched a good discussion of the senses ...

To develop the sense of touch, we blindfolded some volunteers and had them describe objects they were feeling without actually naming them. For sound, we wrote thoughts to music and tape-recorded sounds. For development of sight, I first prepared a slide show of famous paintings and described how to look for such elements as shape, design, perspective, texture, movement, lighting, and color. Students began to really look at and analyze these works with a critical eye. ...

Dr. Nancy Larrick suggests additional ways to involve children in the sensory approach to writing poetry ("Let's Do Poetry," Scholastic elementary magazines, teacher edition, November 9, 1970, p. 3):

Often it helps to bring in familiar objects which children can handle and then record their thoughts about ... anything small enough to pick up and see from every angle. One group of fifth graders soon set up what they called a "junk tray" from which they chose the inspiration for poetic images, even short poems ...

In another class, wire coat hangers were twisted into modern sculpture which led to poetry writing.

After children have had such sensory experiences, they can be encouraged to look for poems that deal with the senses, and, of course, write their own poems.

SPORTS IN POETRY

Donald Anderson, a sixth-grade teacher in Las Vegas, Nevada, whets his students' poetry appetites with a sports in poetry bulletin board display.

A photo montage about a specific sport (baseball, football, water skiing) along with several related sports poems is created by the students. On the bulletin board is the following suggestion: "Make a photo montage yourself about a sport you like. Find a poem about the sport. Or write one yourself."

Underneath the bulletin board are several books containing sports poems. Three sources for upper grades are *Sprints and Distances: Sports in Poetry and Poetry in Sports* (T. Y. Crowell, 1965) compiled by Lillian Morrison, *Sports Poems* (Dell, 1971, pap.), edited by R. R. Knudson and P. K. Ebert, the below mentioned *Faces and Places: Poems for You* (Scholastic Book Services), and *Hosannah, the Home Run!: Poems about Sports* (Little, Brown, 1972), selected by Alice Fleming. Almost every sport is represented in *Sprints and Distances*. Included are poems by ancient and modern writers ranging from Virgil to David McCord. The text is suited for mature readers. *Sports Poems* is a collection of over a hundred poems by such authors as Cassius Clay, Carl Sandburg, and Emily Dickinson. The volume is divided into three sections: "Major Sports," "Minor Sports," and "Losers/Winners." An interesting feature of this anthology is the inclusion of facts and figures about sports events under the heading "Hall of Fame." Here is a book that will have strong appeal to older readers. *Faces and Places* contains a section "Sports and Games"; ten poems by contemporary poets are included. The poems are directed to children in grades four and up. *Hosannah, the Home Run!* includes thirty-four poems about fourteen popular sports. The volume is illustrated with black and white action photos.

STYROFOAM AND SPACE POEM PROJECTS

A study of space can tie in with current events and man's explorations while presenting some excellent poetry. After girls and boys have heard, read, or written poems about space, encourage them to do a display. Give each child a small styrofoam ball and have him paint it with tempera paint. Next, provide him with round, colored toothpicks. These are easily inserted into the styrofoam. The finished products can be attached to a bulletin board display featuring poems, current events clippings from newspapers and magazines, and children's original artwork. Several of the balls might be strung together to create hanging mobiles.

A variety of space poems appears in the "Space and Space and Space..." section in *Faces and Places: Poems for You,* (available in paperback from Scholastic Book Services), selected by Lee Bennett Hopkins and Misha Arenstein, and in *Poems of Earth and Space* (Dutton, 1967) by Claudia Lewis.

FOR FURTHER READING

Cullum, Albert. *Push Back the Desks.* New York: Citation Press, 1967.

The chapter "Poetry Pot" cites specific ideas on using poetry with children throughout the grades.

Herbert, Edward. "On the Teaching of Poetry," *English Journal,* April 1965, p. 334.

The author describes how he led his class from a discussion of baseball to poetry by asking students to list baseball phrases that had become a part of our everyday language such as "He's in there pitching" and "He had to throw in the towel!" Explaining these terms led to paraphrasing and student awareness that paraphrasing was less concrete and dramatic than the original. This led into a discussion of imagery in general and finally, imagery in poetry.

Hopkins, Lee Bennett. *Let Them Be Themselves: Language Arts Enrichment for Disadvantaged Children in Elementary Schools.* New York: Citation Press, 1969.

The chapter "Poetry: Happiness Falling from the Sky!" relates practical experiences of teachers who have enriched children's lives through poetry. Audiovisual aids, suggested readings, and an appendix of "Outstanding Volumes of Black Poetry" also are given.

"Picturing Poetry," *The Instructor,* March 1971, pp. 96–7.

One idea is presented that can spark an exciting poetry project. Children's full-color artwork is used to illustrate six poems, all reprinted. Poems include John Ciardi's "Poor Little Fish," Phyllis McGinley's "C is for Circus," and Eleanor Farjeon's "Mrs. Peck-Pigeon."

Rathbone, Charles. "Prelude to the Making of a Poem: Finger Exercises," *English Journal,* December 1965, pp. 851–6.

"Poetry is words singing: the rhythm and roll of the line . . . the flowing or jolt of individual words spoken in a special way. . . ."

The role of the teacher, according to the author, is to make students sensitive to sounds without further antagonizing them. Rathbone provides many excellent, practical suggestions to use with children. For example, he asked his class to make a list of a dozen words for a category—herbs and spices, detergents, automobile parts, girls' names—and then arrange several of the words so that when read aloud they sounded poetic. Many, many ideas, to use on any grade level in this check-plus article.

Schmidlin, Lois Nelson. "Introducing Two-Word Poetry," *The Instructor*, May 1970, pp. 53–4.

A former fourth-grade teacher from Nevada describes how she got her students turned on with two-word poetry, two words per line. A good technique for children who say they can't!

LET'S BURY THE FAIRIES

POETRY REFLECTING
CONTEMPORARY TRENDS

Children living in the 1970's are *now* children. They are the children who have lived through the turbulent decade of the 1960's, experiencing assassinations of world leaders, a war that nobody understands, cities in crisis, and changes of all kinds from the space boom to X-rated films shown in local movie houses.

Years ago headlines such as those about the Charles Manson murder trial or the controversies sparked by the Lt. Calley case would have been hushed or hidden from youngsters. Today, such news cannot be hidden from them. They see what is happening now *now*—right in their own living rooms via television screens. The composer-musician Bob Dylan certainly is right on when he says, "The times they are a-changin' "—they are a-changin'—daily!

On the afternoon of November 22, 1963, boys and girls may have witnessed President John F. Kennedy attending a parade in his honor in Dallas, Texas. Three days later they viewed the somber procession of his military funeral. Is it any wonder that today's youth are highly individualistic, that they want the world of today to be today? As adults, we often forget that it is today. We turn to the past—our past—because it is familiar, even safer perhaps. But children do not thrive on the past. They hunger for now and for what the future will bring.

Recently in a New York City classroom, a fourth-grade teacher was about to discuss pond life. "Who can give me a

137

definition of the word *pond?*" she asked. One student immediately answered, "Pond is a cold cream. My mother uses it on her face at night before she goes to bed." Here was a child who had never seen a pond. But if he had been asked what marijuana or heroine was, he could probably have provided a lengthy and excellent description.

In a speech given at Lehigh University's 18th Annual Reading Conference, "What the Heart Knows Today" (which appears in Nancy Larrick's *Somebody Turned on a Tap in These Kids: Poetry and Young People Today,* Delacorte, 1971), Myra Cohn Livingston commented:

It is time, I believe, to throw out an entire body of poetry that is no longer meaningful to children, either because of its archaic diction or because it, like its age, concentrated on a point of view, an experience which does not relate to our times. There are still in the classrooms of today many of the same old saws, dragged out decade after decade, which not only fail to engage our children's hearts but build up a horror of . . . poetry; poems of sentimentality for bygone eras, poems of didactic exhortations, poems which extol a world our children will never know and to which they cannot relate, poems of experiences a child has never felt."

Does this mean, then, that we should throw away all the great words that past poets have written? Of course it doesn't. It does mean that if we are to make use of the past, we should make it relevant to the now. In the same speech, Mrs. Livingston goes on to describe how she truly tuned in a group of girls and boys by sharing three related selections: Simon and Garfunkel's song "At the Zoo," a selection from Walt Whitman's *Leaves of Grass* that begins:

> I think I could turn and live with animals,
>   they are so placid and self-contain'd,
> I stand and look at them long and long;

and finally some of Pablo Neruda's "Bestiary."

In this same volume edited by Nancy Larrick, the poet Eve Merriam in her speech, " 'I', Says the Poem," advises: "Avoid the kind of thing (in poetry) where one has fairies creating things rather than nature. Nature is better than any fairy that anybody ever made up."

Many of us were raised on fairies. Fairies were once a popular theme in poetry. And weren't there fairies for *everything?* Fairies were around to let the sunshine in, to make it rain or snow, to make us happy, and to soothe our childhood problems. But fairies don't work too well in the 1970's, and I truly wonder how well they worked in past decades. Any child knows today that it takes more than one fairy to separate the umbilical cord from a rocket ship as it blasts off from its launching pad on its way to the moon. And many boys and girls of pre-school age can discuss phenomena such as the water cycle or the reasons for seasonal change far better than their grandparents could do in their teens.

Our now children want the *now.* And they should receive it from us. If we don't provide it for them, their own poets will —poets like Johnny Cash who asks in his song, "What Is Truth?":

> A little boy of three sittin' on the floor
> Looks up and says, "Daddy, what is war?"
> "Son, that's when people fight and die."
> The little boy of three says, "Daddy, why?"*

If you are not familiar with such poetry, discover it right away via three popular paperback titles: *Favorite Pop/Rock Lyrics, Pop/Rock Lyrics 2,* and *Pop/Rock Lyrics 3,* and *Pop/ Rock Songs of the Earth,* all edited by Jerry L. Walker (all Scholastic Book Services), or go to your nearest newsstand and

---

*© Copyright 1970 by *House of Cash.* Reprinted by permission of the publisher, *House of Cash.*

buy a copy of the monthly magazine *Song Hits*. You will find that the lyrics to these songs are a far cry from "Hiawatha" and "The Village Blacksmith," but they are the words our children are hearing, listening to, memorizing, and singing day after day after day.

Even the youngest child doesn't want poetry from the past, poetry that does not ring of the sounds he knows or wants to hear. This is one reason children are so fond of contemporary poets' work, why they clamor for Dr. Seuss.

Three contemporary themes that recur in poetry for today's children are the city, multi-ethnic experiences, and war and peace.

THE CITY

The city has always been a vital, spirited place. It was written about poetically as early as 1855 when Walt Whitman, the Brooklyn printer, wrote and printed *Leaves of Grass*. He wrote:

> This is the city...and I am one of the citizens;
> Whatever interests the rest interests me...
> Give me such shows—give me the streets of
>   Manhattan!
> Give me Broadway....

In the early part of the twentieth century, Carl Sandburg's *Chicago* (Holt, 1916) and *Smoke and Steel* (Harcourt, 1920) appeared. A few years later a young black man, Langston Hughes, began to write about the ways of life as he lived it and saw it from his home in Harlem.

Many volumes of poetry about the city were issued in the

1960's and 1970's. Now, for the first time, volumes of poetry for children are beginning to appear due in part to increased efforts to solve the cities and the need to revitalize these centers of life and growth. Poems about fire escapes, fire hydrants, and subway systems are rapidly being added to the myriad poems about Queen Anne's lace and dandelion patches.

The selected lists below cite some of the best anthologies and collections of original poems that have grown out of the unrest, decay, and human vitality that prevail among city dwellers.

FOR PRIMARY GRADES

Bissett, Donald J., comp. *Poetry and Verse for Urban Children,* 3 vols. San Francisco: Chandler Publishing Company, 1967, 1968.

Titles in this three-volume series, in paperbound editions, include *Poems and Verses to Begin On, Poems and Verses about Animals,* and *Poems and Verses about the City.* Each volume contains "Hints for Reading Poetry Aloud" and suggestions for using various selections. The poetry is geared to the very young child.

Brooks, Gwendolyn. *Bronzeville Boys and Girls.* New York: Harper and Row, 1956.

These original poems for young readers offer an engaging look into the lives of children living in the crowded conditions of an American innercity. Gwendolyn Brooks is the first black poet to receive a Pulitzer Prize for Poetry. Drawings are by Ronni Solbert.

Hoffman, Hilde. *The City and Country Mother Goose.* New York: American Heritage Press, 1969.

Over a hundred color illustrations are included in this contemporary version of Mother Goose. The text can be used to spark creative writing with older students.

141

Hopkins, Lee Bennett, comp. *The City Spreads Its Wings*. New York: Franklin Watts, 1970.

Subways and hot dog vendors, streets and machines, and people young and old—at work, at play—are written about by such master poets as Langston Hughes, Gwendolyn Brooks, Carl Sandburg, and Myra Cohn Livingston. The anthology, illustrated by Moneta Barnett, reflects the moods, people, weather, and special places that the city holds for young children.

————. *I Think I Saw a Snail: Young Poems for City Seasons*. New York: Crown, 1969.

Nineteen poems and profuse illustrations reflect the city in its changing seasons. Black and white sketches by Harold James capture the city's children as well as her many moods.

————. *This Street's for Me!* New York: Crown, 1970.

Seventeen original poems reflecting the special image in the life of a city child—riding the subway, playing "Fire-Escape Follow-the-Leader," and experiencing the *splash! ker-plash!* of the open fire hydrant. Two-color illustrations are by Ann Grifalconi.

Moore, Lilian. *I Feel the Same Way*. New York: Atheneum, 1967 (also available in paperback from Scholastic Book Services); *I Thought I Heard the City*, Atheneum, 1969.

Twenty poems are contained in *I Feel the Same Way*; seventeen in *I Thought I Heard the City*. Mrs. Moore's poems speak of the usual and unusual aspects of city living. The hardcover edition of *I Feel the Same Way* is illustrated by Robert Quackenbush; the paperback by Beatrice Darwin. Mary Jane Dunton has created collages for *I Thought I Heard the City*. Both volumes will appeal to younger girls and boys.

Ridlon, Marci. *That Was Summer*. New York: Follett, 1969.

Forty-nine poems portray the urban environment in this truly refreshing volume. The poet sees not only the fun and excitement of city living but its ugliness and loneliness as well.

FOR UPPER-ELEMENTARY GRADES

Adoff, Arnold, ed. *City in All Directions.* New York: Macmillan, 1969 (also available in paperback).

Eighty-one poems written over the past fifty years are included in this anthology. Poets include Langston Hughes, Lawrence Ferlinghetti, May Swanson, e. e. cummings, and Yevgeny Yevtushenko. Drawings by Donald Carrick add to the tone of the volume, which will have special appeal to mature readers. Notes on some of the selections serve as brief biographies of the poets.

Hopkins, Lee Bennett, comp. *City Talk.* New York: Alfred A. Knopf, 1970.

The forty-two cinquain poems were written by children living in and around urban centers. The text is illustrated with Roy Arenella's black and white photographs.

Larrick, Nancy, ed. *I Heard a Scream in the Streets: Poetry by Young People in the City.* New York: M. Evans, 1970 (also available in paperback from Bantam).

From more than 5,000 poems by young people in twenty-three American cities, Dr. Larrick selected seventy-seven for this anthology. The text is handsomely illustrated with prize-winning photographs selected from the annual Scholastic-Kodak Photography Awards.

————. *On City Streets.* New York: M. Evans, 1969 (also available in paperback from Bantam).

This anthology, compiled with the help of more than a hundred city youngsters of mixed ethnic and socio-economic backgrounds, reflects urban sights and sounds that speak to all children of today's world. The works of over fifty poets appear in this timely and handsomely designed volume. Dramatic black and white photographs by David Sagarin depict the city's many moods.

Lewis, Richard. *The Park.* New York: Simon and Schuster, 1968.

A city park is portrayed during the changing seasons of the

year. The reader is taken on a journey through the words of a poet and the keen photographic eye of Helen Buttfield.

Merriam, Eve. *The Inner City Mother Goose.* New York: Simon and Schuster, 1969 (also available in paperback edition).

This poet-extraordinaire has used Mother Goose rhymes to bite, sting, and underline the horrors that exist in the city. She pulls no punches. The book is designed with black and white visuals by Lawrence Ratzkin. For mature readers.

Schonborg, Virginia. *Subway Swinger.* New York: Morrow, 1970.

Twenty-six poems reflecting children's interests in and reactions to the urban environment are presented. The author, who has also provided the pen and ink illustrations, is a faculty member of the Bank Street College of Education in New York City.

MULTI-ETHNIC EXPERIENCES

THE BLACK EXPERIENCE

During the 1960's America witnessed many civil rights movements, such as sit-ins, voter registration drives, and efforts to desegregate the schools throughout the country, which gained widespread recognition of blacks in every aspect of life. The impact of these movements prompted the publishing of material portraying the cultural heritage of blacks and the black experience. Prior to the 1960's few volumes of poetry written by or about such experiences appeared. The list below cites some of the best collections of original poems and anthologies, most of which were published in the 1960's and 1970's. The titles are mainly geared for children in the upper-grades; however, you will find poems within the volumes that can be used with younger children.

FOR PRIMARY GRADES

Brooks, Gwendolyn, *Bronzeville Boys and Girls*. New York: Harper and Row, 1956.
See annotation in "The City" list earlier in this chapter.

Clifton, Lucille. *Some of the Days of Everett Anderson; Everett Anderson's Christmas Coming*. New York: Holt, 1970, 1971 (also available in paperback).
These are two of the few books for young children that tenderly portrays the `black experience in poetry. The poems tell about six-year-old Everett Anderson who lives in Apt. 14A. Everett plays in the rain, is afraid of the dark, feels lonely, and wonders about things. The texts are beautifully illustrated in line and wash drawings by Caldecott Award winning artist, Evaline Ness. Miss Clifton is a new black poet whose work can be compared to Gwendolyn Brooks.

Giovanni, Nikki. *Spin a Soft Black Song: Poems for Children*. New York: Hill and Wang, 1971.
The young, black poet Nikki Giovanni and illustrator Charles Bible "decided to write a book with poems and pictures for and about children 'cause when we were growing up there were precious few of them." The poems in the book speak about universal thoughts—"shopping," "mommies," "daddies," "fear." The poems, however, are not as good nor as strong in feeling as Gwendolyn Brooks' *Bronzeville Boys and Girls*.

FOR UPPER-ELEMENTARY GRADES

Adoff, Arnold. *Black Out Loud: An Anthology of Modern Poems by Black Americans*. New York: Macmillan, 1970.
In this collection Mr. Adoff presents works of promising young poets as well as those of such mature artists as Langston Hughes, LeRoi Jones, and Margaret Walker. This is the first anthology of this type to be published since 1941, when Arna Bontemps presented *Golden Slippers* (see below).

In his preface the editor comments: "They write of love, hatred, protest, and pride. They write of joy and anger of life in our country . . . The poets are among the change-makers. They have seen themselves. They have seen their people and their country. And they have created fine poems to say and sing and shout what they feel and know and want." Black and white drawings are by Alvin Hollingsworth. Brief biographical notes are also included.

————. *I Am the Darker Brother.* New York: Macmillan, 1968 (also available in paperback).

Mature readers will enjoy this anthology of modern poems written by black Americans. Many of the selections speak of, and for, innercity inhabitants. Notes on several of the poems appear as well as brief biographies of the poets.

Bontemps, Arna, comp. *Golden Slippers: An Anthology of Negro Poetry for Young Readers.* New York: Harper and Row, 1941.

Here is a first! Selections include poetry by such poets as Paul Laurence Dunbar, Claude McKay, Countee Cullen, and Langston Hughes as well as traditional and spiritual ballads and slave songs. Twenty-two drawings by Henrietta Sharon make this volume one for all ages as well as a collector's item.

Hopkins, Lee Bennett, comp. *Don't You Turn Back: Poems by Langston Hughes.* New York: Alfred A. Knopf, 1969.

Forty-five poems by the poet laureate of the black people are included. The introduction by Arna Bontemps speaks of the universality of Hughes' words. Two-color woodcuts are by Ann Grifalconi. The volume can be used with children of all ages.

Hughes, Langston, ed. *New Negro Poets: U.S.A.* Bloomington: Indiana University Press, 1964 (also available in paperback).

Mature students can read the poems in this anthology. Biographical notes are included on the poets.

Jordan, June, ed. *Soulscript: Afro-American Poetry.* New York: Doubleday (also available in paperback).

For mature readers, this collection features the work of black master poets. A section "Hero Hymns and Heroines" includes poems about Malcolm X, Harriet Tubman, and Frederick Douglass that can tie in with American history.

————. *Who Look at Me.* New York: T. Y. Crowell, 1969.

This long, narrative poem for mature readers is enhanced by twenty-seven extraordinary paintings of American life, many reproduced in full color. Notes about the artists are included.

Merriam, Eve. *I Am a Man: Ode to Martin Luther King, Jr.* New York: Doubleday, 1971.

Although this is a picture book, the simple evocative poem will appeal to older students. The ode ends, "*I am a man.* Now he was gone./The dream and the freedom road lead on." Illustrations are by Suzanne Verrier.

AMERICAN INDIANS AND ESKIMOS

The American Indian and the problems they face in American society have also become an area of social concern today. Poetry of and by the American Indian and Eskimo is appearing on the scene. There are fewer volumes of Indian poetry than there are volumes dealing with urban life and the black experience, but several fine collections have recently been published to preserve and teach the rich culture of Indian life. Future years will undoubtedly bring additional titles. The books listed below can best be read by upper-grade children; however, many can be shared with children in the lower grades.

FOR UPPER GRADES

Bierheist, John, ed. *In the Trails of the Winds: American Indian Poems and Ritual Orations.* New York: Farrar, Straus and Giroux, 1971.

This volume includes 126 poems translated from over forty languages and representing all the best-known Indian cultures of North and South America. Omens, battle songs, orations, love lyrics, prayers, dreams, and mystical incantations appear, beginning with the origin of the earth and the emergence of man through to the apocalyptic visions of a new life. Detailed notes appear on each of the selections along with "Suggestions for Further Reading" and a "Glossary of Tribes, Cultures, and Languages," which give great insight into the poetry. The volume is illustrated with black and white period engravings.

Concha, Joseph L. *Lonely Deer: Poems by a Pueblo Indian Boy.* (Available in paperback edition from Red Willow Society, Box 1184, Taos, New Mexico 87571.)

This don't-miss book was written by a young, seventeen-year-old poet, the third of four children in the family of Alex and Mary Concha. His birthplace was the high mesa of Taos, New Mexico, where the roots planted by his forebearers have been at one with the soil for more than 800 years. Constantine Aiello, one of Joseph's teachers, encouraged him to write the poetry contained within this small volume. Most of the poems are about nature: "Twilight on the Prairie," "Aspens," "Colored Rocks," are several of the titles. Also contains three design-paintings done by the poet.

Jones, Hettie, comp. *The Trees Stand Shining.* New York: Dial, 1971.

This volume will appeal to young children because of its format. It is a large, picture book containing beautiful, full-color paintings by Robert Andrew, 1970 Caldecott Honor Book winner. The anthologist arranged this collection to trace a journey through two day's times; she tells the reader that. "The poems . . . are really songs . . . In their songs, American Indians told how they felt about the world, all they saw in the land, what they did in their lives." The songs are from such tribes as the Iroquois, Teton Sioux, Chipewa, and Papago.

Lewis, Richard, ed. *I Breathe a New Song: Poems of the Eskimo.*
New York: Simon and Schuster, 1971.

This handsome anthology grew out of the anthologist's interest
in the literature of indigenous peoples. Mr. Lewis states in his
editor's note: "My hope is that this collection will help preserve
a culture that began to disappear in 1955, when encounter with
modern technology, information, and life patterns began to destroy Eskimo life as it had been lived for over 1,300 years ..."
Bold, graphic illustrations by Oonark compliment this rich volume;
the introduction by the anthropologist, Edmund Carpenter, describes
the people, their beliefs, and their ways of forming poetry.

WAR AND PEACE

Years ago Carl Sandburg told of a small girl who, after
hearing him describe one of the Civil War battles, said, "Sup-
pose they gave a war and no one came?" Unfortunately, that
day is yet to come! Today's boys and girls know about war.
War surrounds us. It is talked about, read about, and seen daily
on television screens the country over. Fighting wars, and the
threats of future wars, are troubling every nation.

On October 15, 1969, *moratorium* became a household word.
Boys and girls of all ages wanted to know the meaning of the
word. What, why, how, who, and when questions concerning
Vietnam pored from their lips. In a fifth-grade class in Scarsdale, a wealthy community in New York State, a child created
a simple poem:

> Boys are dying,
> Mothers are crying.
> Why do we have war?

In Harlem, another fifth-grader wrote a cinquain poem:

> War is—
> Bullets and guns
> Fighting and killing with
> Little living and much dying.
> The end.

These two children, miles apart on a socio-economic scale, thought many of the same thoughts. They worry about war because war is an integral part of their everyday lives.

Poems about war are appearing more and more in books of poetry for children. In Eve Merriam's *Finding a Poem* (Atheneum, 1970), there are several biting poems on the theme. "Fantasia" consists of only fifteen words but leaves the reader shuddering with goose bumps. It tells of a woman who dreams of giving birth to a child—"a child/who will ask/'Mother,/what was war?'" "The Dirty Words" and "And Son" are others in the collection.

Mature readers can feel the sting of Langston Hughes' words about war in his last volume of poetry (published posthumously) *The Panther and the Lash* (Alfred A. Knopf, 1967; also available in paperback); section four, "The Face of War," includes seven poems.

Two other anthologies for mature readers that include poems about war are *Sounds and Silences: Poetry for Now* (Dell, 1970; also available in paperback), edited by Richard Peck, and *To Play Man Number One: Poems of Modern Man* (Atheneum, 1969), compiled by Sara Hannum and John Terry Chase.

In the first volume ten poems are given in a chapter entitled "War." They include Gwendolyn Brooks' "The Sonnett-Ballad," Pete Seeger's stirring lyrics to "Where Have All the Flowers Gone?" and e. e. cummings' poignant poem "my sweet old etcetera."

To Play Man Number One contains fourteen poems in the section "A Million People on One String: The Tragedy of War." Archibald MacLeish's "What the Old Women Say" and Karl Shapiro's "The Leg" are two of the selections. Erwin Schachner's strong illustrations add to this excellent anthology.

When children hear or read such poetry as the above, they don't seem to feel alone with their thoughts. Far too often, boys and girls, particularly young ones, are not listened to or heard when they bring up the subject of war. Yet children themselves talk about war. A ten year old recently asked his father, "If Vietnam doesn't end in eight years, can we move to Canada?" And a third-grade child, after hearing about Lt. Calley, remarked, "He killed babies. But they were all bad babies. They weren't Americans."

Children, too, are expressing themselves about war in poetry. In his book *The Bright Red Porcupine* (Harlin Quist, 1969), the young twelve-year-old poet Tony Cavin writes a poem asking why, "Millions of schoolchildren/[are]/Killed every week/ As they gaily trot off to school."

Aliki Barnstone was only twelve-years-old when her book, *The Real Tin Flower* (Crowell-Collier, 1968), was published. In this volume war is the subject of two of her poems: "On Memorial Day: For Sappho and Greek Democracy" and "The War."

Children's voices are also heard in chapter three of *Here I Am! An Anthology of Poems Written by Young People in Some of America's Minority Groups* (Dutton, 1969; also available in paperback from Bantam), edited by Virginia Olsen Baron. In the book Juanita Bryant tells us "The World's Coming to an End;" Michael Goode writes "April 4, 1968," beginning his poem: "war war/why do God's children fight among each other/like animals..."

I Never Saw Another Butterfly (Simon and Schuster, 1964), edited by M. Volovkova, contains drawings and poems that were found at Terezin in German-occupied Czechoslovakia. They were all created by girls and boys. During World War II, some 15,000 young people were sent to this Nazi camp where more than 40,000 Jews were crowded into a town where only 7,000 had previously lived. Terezin was the last stop before death. The children's drawings and poems reflect the tragedy of their lives; but as children, many also depicted what adults could no longer see. They wrote of and drew the beauty of the surrounding countryside and they drew imaginative drawings of princesses and clowns. Of the 15,000 who were sent to Terezin, only a hundred children lived to see the war's end. The book is a testimony to the creative young people who were put to death by the Nazis.

Two recently published paperbacks that contain children's writings are: *The Children: Poems and Prose from Bedford-Stuyvesant* (Grove Press, 1971), edited by Irving Beling, and *Peace Is You and Me: Children's Writings and Paintings on Love and Peace* (Avon Books, 1971), collected by Florence Weiner.

The writings in *The Children* are bitter comments about life in the ghetto. The volume is divided into eight sections, the last being "There Is Killing Going on in Vietnam." The poems are not particularly good but do offer the thoughts of angry, upper-grade children.

Peace Is You and Me is a far better collection. Mrs. Weiner wrote to peace centers and schools across the country asking them to send the personal feelings children had expressed about war and peace. The results are in this attractive paperback. The anthologist has also included an annotated bibliography of books with a theme of peace and bettering the world, and lists books for use throughout the grades—from pre-school through college—along with a helpful listing of peace organizations.

FOR FURTHER READING

Griffith, Winthrop. "The Taos Have a Small Generation Gap," *New York Times Magazine,* February 21, 1971, pp. 26–7, 93–7 +.

Both generations of the Taos Pueblo in New Mexico find meaning in a one-thousand-year-old heritage. The article tells of the strength of Taos culture derived from the beauty of the sacred Blue Lake lands, recently returned to the Indians by the United States government.

Hopkins, Lee Bennett. "Negro Poets: Through the Music of Their Words," *Elementary English,* February, 1968, pp. 206–8.

Brief biographies and samples of the work of Langston Hughes, Paul Laurence Dunbar, and Gwendolyn Brooks are presented.

Johnson, Thomas A. "Renaissance in Black Poetry Expresses Anger," *New York Times,* April 25, 1969, pp. 49, 94.

Contemporary black poets including LeRoi Jones, Nikki Giovanni, Gylan Kain, June Jordan, and others are discussed.

From *Pick a Peck O'Poems*, © 1972, by Miller-Brody Productions Inc.

TO SEE AND HEAR AND FEEL:
POETRY IN MEDIA

The media boom is definitely upon us. Unfortunately, however, few poetry materials are available for presentation to children.

This chapter describes the best that is around. Materials with which children can produce their own media is discussed at the end. Items mentioned in previous chapters are not described again here.

LIVE PRESENTATION

Poetry like music is meant to be heard! There is no better way to acquaint children with poetry than through live presentations. One of the best programs in the country that is available to schools is Periwinkle Productions. This is live theater that truly excites the imagination of children. The dynamic founder and producer of Periwinkle Productions is Sunna Rasch whose background embraces both education and the theater. She has created three unique and unforgettable programs for boys and girls of all ages: *The Magic Word* for primary youngsters; *Poetry in 3-D* for middle-grade children; *Poetry Now* for junior and senior high schools. All three of the programs feature a professional, integrated company of Equity actors and actresses. Additional programs are being prepared.

In *The Magic Word* four characters explore a wonderland of fantasy as a father and his two daughters encounter the Spirit of Poetry in the middle of the forest. The Spirit whisks them off to the Land of Poetry-Magic. In the course of the production, each traveler experiences his own awakening. The father learns that a person is never too old to smile or to grow. His children discover there is a world within themselves. And the Spirit accomplishes her mission—she has touched the imagination of each child in the audience!

The production has bigger-than-life-sized props and colorful costumes and invites the children in the audience to recite nursery rhymes, sing, count, and have a Periwinkle-good time.

Poetry in 3-D offers children the opportunity to learn about other people and discusses both tangible and intangible ideas; it leaves children enthused about poetry so that they will turn to it as a means of expression and be motivated to read and search for more poetry.

The program uses dialogue, props, and costumes, while skillfully presenting familiar poems to the audience. Selections include poems by Edward Lear, Lewis Carroll, Langston Hughes, and e. e. cummings as well as a series of Japanese haiku.

Poetry Now is a dramatic presentation of verse for today's with-it youth. The poetry ranges from Shakespeare to pop-rock lyrics by Simon and Garfunkel. The program reaches children of all socio-economic levels. With just four actors in four chairs and a prop or two, a continuous script flows like a gentle stream.

Carol Cherkis, Director of the College Bound Program with New York's Board of Education, remarked in a letter to the producer:

Poetry Now serves as a cultural bond between the Now and the Then; and in that respect tends to serve as a cementing agent between the generations. It helps our young to see that good things were happening in the world before the 1970's; and it helps adults to see that the young can and do appreciate what is fresh, sincere, and pertinent to their lives.

Prior to each production, schools are sent a study kit for teachers, which cites the production's contents and gives excellent ideas for motivation and follow-up. The various programs have been presented throughout the country. Productions range in cost from $300 to $400 within one hundred miles of New York City. Prices will be quoted on request for areas outside this radius. Series' rates, which include transportation, are also available on request. The programs are available under Federal funding, Titles I and III.

I've seen Periwinkle Productions in which young and old audiences were transfixed by the words and actions of the players. I got goose bumps, laughed, felt badly, and felt good along with hundreds of boys and girls, all of whom felt the same way.

You can write for further program information and descriptive literature to Sunna Rasch, Periwinkle Productions, 19 Clinton Avenue, Monticello, New York 12701.

MOTHER GOOSE IN MEDIA

Mother Goose has been treated in a number of unique ways in media. The following materials are those that have proved to be most effective with children and their teachers.

RECORDINGS AND MULTI-MEDIA SETS

Caedmon Records (distributed by D. C. Heath and Company, features a twelve-inch LP album *Mother Goose.* It stars three luminaries from the entertainment world, Cyril Ritchard, Celeste Holm, and Boris Karloff, who perform sixty-nine verses and songs. The material is also available on two-track, seven-inch tapes and cassettes.

Scholastic Book Services has two delightful book-record combinations. *Hi Diddle Diddle* features thirty-seven rhymes in song, verse, and music on a seven-inch LP recording. The set includes a picture paperback volume of forty-two rhymes with illustrations by Nola Langner. *Mother Ghost Nursery Rhymes and Other Tricks and Treats* contains a seven-inch LP recording containing a collection of scary rhymes and the classic children's story *Georgie,* the friendly little ghost who can't even scare a mouse. Each set is packaged together in a sturdy folder.

Spoken Arts, Inc., has produced two record albums called *Treasury of Nursery Rhymes.* The selections are sung, read, and arranged by Christopher Casson, the son of Dame Sybil Thorndike and Sir Lewis Casson. Volume I contains fifty-three rhymes featuring such characters as Wee Willie Winkie, Jack and Jill, and Old Mother Goose herself. Volume II contains fifty-one selections.

To enhance the songs, Mr. Casson uses an Irish harp and recorder for pleasing backgrounds. Many of the rhymes on these recordings have also been used in a multi-media package that includes four records, four filmstrips, four teachers' guides, and spirit master activity sheets for the youngsters. The color filmstrips get children involved in singing and participating in the rhymes. For the most part, the set features Mother Goose melodies; however, ballads, folk songs, street cries, prayers, rituals, and proverbs are also included. A particularly pleasing selection is "The First Day of Christmas." Most of the material can be used to develop awareness of numbers, color, and size relationships.

The brief teachers' guides offer suggestions for before viewing and after viewing; a vocabulary review is also included. The spirit master student activity sheets add little to the package and are quite incidental. The company's catalog cites price information.

Bowmar features two complete programs of Mother Goose —*Mother Goose Songs* and *Children's Songs*. Each program is made up of familiar nursery rhymes. Each includes: eight full-color, art-study prints, 22 x 29 inches, which have teaching suggestions on the reverse side grouped under three headings: The Picture and the Rhyme, Phrase Strips and Word Study, and Activities and Extensions; eight cards, 22 x 29 inches with the first verse of each rhyme in manuscript that is large and easily read by children; eight perforated cards, 22 x 29 inches, with which to make phrase or sentence strips of the first verse of each rhyme; two filmstrips, each combining art work and rhymes from four of the songs; one record presenting music; and ten paperback minibooks, 4 x 6 inches, each containing the rhymes and accompanying art prints in color. Write for a descriptive brochure for further details and for the cost of the programs.

FILMS AND POSTERS

McGraw-Hill Films has produced two excellent motion pictures based on Mother Goose rhymes in their "Storybook Series": *Old Mother Hubbard and Her Dog* and *The House that Jack Built.* Each film is four minutes long and is in full color; they are based on the books and artwork of the same titles by the delightful Paul Galdone.

Hubbard Press has recently published a handsome volume, *The Classic Volland Edition of Mother Goose.* The book contains 110 full-page, four-color illustrations by Fred Richardson.

Hubbard also offers two visual-aid picture sets, *Mother Goose,* sets 1 and 2, based on this text. Each set contains ten full-color, 9 x 12-inch pictures printed on high quality stock; they are the best of the Mother Goose posters. Put them on your must Mother Goose list!

AUDIO AND VISUAL MATERIALS

FILMS

Children in upper-elementary grades can be introduced to poets of yore via seven films in *The Living Poetry* series produced by McGraw-Hill. These color films use original artwork and music to enhance dramatic readings and encourage students to read the originals. Films in the series are:

Poems of Walt Whitman includes four poems: "I Hear America Singing," "Miracles," "When I Heard the Learn'd Astronomer," and "O Captain! My Captain!"

Poems of Tennyson and Browning: Robert Browning's "Incident of the French Camp" and Alfred Lord Tennyson's "The Charge of the Light Brigade" are included. A teacher's guide provides brief historical backgrounds to the incidents on which these poems were based.

The Deacon's Masterpiece: Oliver Wendell Holmes' poem about the "one-horse shay that lasted one hundred years to the day" is depicted.

Paul Revere's Ride by Henry Wadsworth Longfellow has been a long-time favorite with children. The film version captures the urgency and magnitude of Revere's mission when "the fate of a nation was riding that night . . ."

Casey at the Bat depicts all the excitement and tension of the Mudville nine's valiant try for victory in the bottom of the ninth

—with two away, two men on, and the "mighty Casey" coming to bat. The filmstrip is illustrated with original, stylized drawings that catch the mood of the famous ball game.

Poems of Lewis Carroll: Three poems, "Father William," "The Walrus and the Carpenter," and "The Gardener's Song," illustrate the writer's special wit and humor.

Hiawatha's Childhood is part three of Longfellow's 22-part "The Song of Hiawatha," beginning just after the birth of Hiawatha and continuing to his entrance into manhood.

All of the films run between eight and thirteen minutes and are available for rent or purchase.

Media Plus distributes three ten-minute films and filmstrip-record sets in its *Poetry Is Alive and Well and Living in America* series. The films, for mature students, provide glimpses into the life styles and works of three contemporary poets: May Swenson, Edward Field, and Gloria C. Oden. The best of the three for use with elementary grades is the one featuring May Swenson. The poet is shown at her home in Long Island. She discusses her work, how she writes, what inspires her. Two of her poems are vibrantly illustrated as she reads them: "The Pregnant Dream" is read over a sequence of psychedelic visuals; "Still Turning" concerns a fantasy ride on a merry-go-round. The poems are from her book *Half Sun, Half Sleep* (Scribner 1967). A guide, prepared by Dr. Rozanne Knudson, cites ways of sparking children's thoughts after they view the film and includes the text to the poems.

This series has received excellent reviews. *Media and Methods* commented that the films are "the biggest educational advance in poetry since the death of memorization." A brochure, available free, cites children's own testimonies. One fifth-grader created his own dream after hearing and seeing the film:

My Potato Dream

I had a dream,
About a potato
That was brown,
With a purple crown.

Then I had a dream
A dream of everything.
The dream was purple,
With white and mixed up green.

But this time the potato was
    white with a dot of green.

And this was my dream.

POSTERS

Posters can add a great deal to the classroom, particularly the poetry corner. Posters are all around us today—in store displays, subways and buses, and particularly in children's rooms. Recently the poster has become the in-thing with boys and girls of all ages. Basically, any poster embodies the same basic principles—they immediately catch the eye, hold one's attention, and impress an image upon the senses. All of this is done via good design, a minimum amount of words, large, bold use of color, and attractiveness.

Often more can be taught by one effective poster than can be crammed into several lessons. A child seeing an example of concrete poetry hanging in the room, for instance, grasps the idea of what it is all about; the haiku form is more impressed upon a child's mind if he can see a large illustrated example, than if he reads dozens of haiku poems.

Several poetry posters are available from Scholastic Book Services. *Three Poems Poster Package* contains three poems gaily illustrated by top artists in the children's book field: Christina Rosetti's "Who Has Seen the Wind?," Eleanor Farjeon's "Mrs. Peck Pigeon," and the traditional verse, "Four Seasons." The 22 x 29-inch posters are in full-color and are suited for children in pre-school through grade three.

For the upper-elementary grades *Four Poems Package: Poetry I and Poetry II* are available. Poetry I includes four, two-color, 22 x 17-inch posters showing four different types of poetic forms: Haiku is portrayed by Issa; Robert Francis' "The Base Stealer" shows an example of free verse; a pop-rock poster features the late Jimi Hendrix's lyrics for "Up from the Skies;" and there is an excerpt from the classic poem "Evangeline" by Henry Wadsworth Longfellow.

Poetry II also consists of four, two-color, 22 x 17-inch, diversified posters that emphasize varied forms. The poems include Langston Hughes' "Motto," Reed Whitmore's "The High School Band," Chet Powers' pop-rock lyrics to "Let's Get Together," and Walt Whitman's "When I Heard the Learn'd Astronomer."

RECORDINGS

Recordings of poetry are beneficial because children can hear the spoken word, often of live poets reading their own work. However, if recordings are improperly used, they can quickly destroy a child's appreciation of poetry. One mistake often made is to tell the class they are going to hear a recording of poetry and then play the record from start to finish. No child, no matter how much he likes poetry, can bear listening to a complete recording. Children can only listen to so much—

and so much is very little! Use recordings wisely. Play one or two selections and allow children to savor the voice, words, and rhythms of the poems—then stop. If a child wants to hear more, let him do so—by himself in a corner of the room.

Many companies are placing recordings on cassettes, which are less destructible and easier to handle than discs.

Poetry Parade is a two-record album edited by Nancy Larrick and produced by Weston Woods. The recordings feature four top children's poets reading their own works: David McCord and Harry Behn are on one; Karla Kuskin and Aileen Fisher are on the second. Dr. Larrick introduces each of the poets prior to their reading, giving brief biographical sketches. The album come with a sensible guide, "Using Poetry with Children," in which Dr. Larrick states:

Probably no one wants to hear the entire parade of four poets without time to absorb and respond along the way. In fact, few children will listen appreciatively to an entire side of a record without some breaks for their own participation.

The guide gives specific suggestions for using the records as well as hints for using selected poems. The company's catalog gives price information.

John Ciardi can be heard reading his works specifically written for young audiences and based on his books on two recordings produced by Spoken Arts. On *You Read to Me, I'll Read to You,* Mr. Ciardi reads to his own children—Benn, John, and Myra—and they, in turn, read back to him. After an introduction by the poet, thirty-four poems are presented, including his sure-fire "Mummy Slept Late and Daddy Fixed Breakfast."

On side 1 of *You Know Who: John J. Plenty and Fiddler Dan and Other Poems,* Mr. Ciardi reads twenty-seven poems from the book *You Know Who.* Selections include "Calling

All Cowboys" and "What Someone Said When He Was Spanked on the Day before His Birthday," which are true ear-catchers for youngsters. Side 2, geared to older boys and girls, features several longer poems including "John J. Plenty and Fiddler Dan" and "The King Who Saved Himself From Being Saved."

Caedmon Records (distributed by D. C. Heath) offers a comprehensive anthology of poems and poets entitled *A Gathering of Great Poetry for Children,* selected by Richard Lewis. The two-volume record set features the work of both contemporary poets and poets of yore, ranging from A. A. Milne to Gwendolyn Brooks. Several of the poems are read by the poets themselves—Carl Sandburg, Robert Frost, and T. S. Eliot; others are read by Julie Harris, Cyril Ritchard, and David Wayne.

SLIDES

Slideas is a new product produced cooperatively by Loyola University Press and the Society for Visual Education, Inc. The material consists of five sets of full-color, 2x2-inch slides, twenty per set, each built upon a theme. "Faces and Feelings" shows children and adults expressing moods of joy, wonder, sorrow, and festivity; "Metropolis" depicts urban life, work and leisure, and poverty and affluence in the city; "Season" shows scenes of the four seasons of the year; "Searching" presents scenes depicting moods of loneliness, alienation, hoping, and seeking; "Sharing," includes slides on family, friendship, love, brotherhood, and celebration.

Each set is packaged in a translucent display folder for easy selection and protective storage. The slides in each set are good for stimulating poetry writing on all grade levels. Suggestions for classroom and individual use are included.

165

A great advantage to such a program is that slides can be projected and left showing on the screen until the class, a small group of children, or individual boys and girls have finished with them. Price information and a catalog is available from Loyola University Press.

MULTI-MEDIA SETS

BOOK-RECORD COMBINATIONS

Scholastic Book Services has created a unique series of book-record combinations; each book-record set includes a Scholastic paperback with its own 7-inch LP recording. The book and record fit neatly into the inside pockets of a sturdy folder with an identifying label on the spine.

The following are available for younger children:

Favorite Rhymes from A Rocket in My Pocket.
Side 1 contains nursery rhymes, riddles, and tongue twisters selected from the book by Carl Withers. The reverse side is the word-for-word narration of the English folk tale "Teeny Tiny Woman." The package contains one record, two books.

Over in the Meadow.
Side 2 is the traditional counting rhyme about the animals in the meadow and their young, written by Olive A. Wadsworth. The original jazz score will delight youngsters. The book is illustrated in collage designs by Ezra Jack Keats. Side 1 features the story "Just in Time for the King's Birthday" by E. B. Chance, a tale of how a farmer makes a fine cheese for the king's birthday and runs into problems delivering it. The package contains one record, two books.

Older boys and girls will enjoy:

Selections from Faces and Places: Poems for You.

Excerpts from the book, selected by Lee Bennett Hopkins and Misha Arenstein, are read by Paul Hecht and Jean Richards. Both light and serious verse by Carl Sandburg, John Ciardi, and Myra Cohn Livingston are included.

Selections from The Arrow Book of Poetry.

Twenty-seven poems and limericks are included from the book edited by Ann McGovern. Lewis Carroll, Eve Merriam, and Rosemary and Stephen Vincent Bénet are among the poets represented.

A POETRY UNIT

The Random House School Division recently put together a poetry learning unit entitled *Aware.* The unit contains: activity cards, each containing a small lesson plan for "sense exploration"; track cards, a set of thirty-six cards featuring individual plans for using the *Aware* materials keyed to difficulty and interest areas in the teacher's guide; four poetry booklets, *Sight, Sound, Touch,* and *Taste and Smell,* containing poetry, prose, and art that reflect the sensory experiences the child has when he works with the activity cards; a twenty-minute tape cassette including poetry and sounds such as a horse galloping, wind howling, a jet take-off, and musical selections ranging from African primitive to modern electronic; scent samples, a set of scent-impregnated cards that release odors when scratched with a fingernail; a Braille card produced by the Perkins Institute for the Blind; *First Voices,* four paperback anthologies of poems and pictures for children in the intermediate grades, edited by Geoffrey Summerfield; and a teacher's guide. For further information on this complete poetry program, write for a descriptive brochure.

167

With the exception of Mother Goose melodies, there is little available to introduce poetry via filmstrips to primary-grade children. Because of this, I was asked to work with Miller-Brody Productions, Inc., to produce a series of six filmstrips and recordings designed for children in pre-kindergarten through grade three. The series is entitled *Pick a Peck o' Poems.* Besides presenting boys and girls with poems by contemporary poets woven into a narrative, the strips define poetic terms in simple language.

The first strip, *What Is Poetry?,* introduces the elements of rhyme, free verse, and imagery ("word pictures"), showing similarities and differences. A second strip, *Sing a Song of Cities,* shows how people, travel, play, shop, and build on city streets. A third, *Animals, Animals, Animals,* shows, through poetry, that animals are everywhere—in houses as pets, in jungles, zoos, and in museums—where they are stuffed, of course! The focus of *When It's Cold, When It's Hot, and When It's Not!* is the seasons and weather. Through poems such as Langston Hughes' "April Rain Song" and Gwendolyn Brooks' "Cynthia in the Snow," children see a change of seasons and how they affect their lives. Opposite points of view tell how some poets like the rain, for example, and others express a distaste for it. *Our Earth to Keep* is a plea to keep the earth beautiful. Trees, flowers, birds, and small animals are seen through poets' eyes. The filmstrip is open-ended, encouraging youngsters to write their own poems, "so that many other girls and boys and grown-ups can hear you—and help, too!"

The last strip in the series, *A Poem Belongs to You,* shows that anyone can write poetry and that all poets are different, thus, they see things through different eyes and feelings.

The package also contains an extensive teachers' guide suggesting questions, activities and containing reprints of all the poems heard on the recordings. For further information on the series, write for a descriptive brochure.

If you really want to extend *The Poetic Experience* in upper-elementary grade classrooms, get the set of this name from Guidance Associates. It contains two full-color filmstrips, two twelve-inch LP recordings, and a discussion guide.

Part 1 of *The Poetic Experience* begins by illustrating the basic rudiments of poetry, rhythm, and sound with familiar rhymes of childhood including Mother Goose melodies, street songs, and a selection from Dr. Seuss. The filmstrip then discusses the poet's sensitivity to his working materials—words, rhythm, form, and imagery. Poets range from William Shakespeare to Lawrence Ferlinghetti; their work is well presented through full-color photographs tied together with a fine narration.

Part 2 concentrates on the poet's "ability to translate the strange and to elevate common experiences through the medium of poetry." Again there is a good variety of poets represented: Shakespeare, William Carlos Williams, Countee Cullen, and Marianne Moore.

There is an added bonus at the end of each of the filmstrips —the name and a photograph of each of the poets represented appear in end-frames. The discussion guide gives the teacher background information for each poem.

The Harlem Renaissance and Beyond is another two-part filmstrip-record program available from Guidance Associates which introduces older students to the major black writers of the 1920's. During four brief but important years, 1925 to 1929, a group of writers living in Harlem began to exchange ideas and help each other; their literary output was unique.

Part 1 of the series examines the Harlem Renaissance, pointing out its accomplishments, shortcomings, and the reason for its abrupt end—the crash of the stock market and the removal of financial support. Part 2 follows the course the major black writers have taken since the end of the Renaissance and discusses the beginning of a gradual philosophical division that ultimately affected writers such as Countee Cullen, Gwendolyn Brooks, Richard Wright, and LeRoi Jones.

The set gives students a lasting impression of these major black writers of the Harlem Renaissance and an appreciation of the special and unique qualities of the Harlem community and its people. The filmstrips are illustrated with photographs taken in Harlem and are supplemented with newspaper photographs and prints. Two filmstrips, two 12-inch LP records, and a discussion guide, which includes all the poems and excerpts as well as questions for discussion, follow-up activities, and a bibliography, are included in the set.

STUDY PRINT-RECORD SETS

A Child's World of Poetry is distributed by Society for Visual Education (SVE) and is a stimulating multi-media approach designed to inspire enthusiasm for poetry. Materials are available in two groups: Group 1 contains eight large, full-color photograph posters, 18 x 13-inches with appropriate poems on the reverse side, plus two 12-inch LP banded recordings. There are sixty poems in the first group that will have special appeal to boys and girls in pre-kindergarten through grade three; Group 2 contains forty-four poems for children in intermediate and junior high school grades. The poems in both sets have been selected for literary merit and special appeal to boys and girls.

Each of the prints focuses on a basic theme. Group 1 features: "It's Raining, It's Pouring!" "I Like Pets," "City Sights and Sounds," "Leaves and the Wind," "The Way to Anywhere,"

"The Land of Make-Believe," "We Like to Play," and "All about Me." Group 2 has: "Lincoln—the Spirit of Freedom," "The Open Sea," "It's Spring Again," "Under Western Skies," "Winter White," "Talk About Trees," "Night Magic," and "Towers to the Sky."

The poetry selections appear on the back of each print along with good questions and suggestions for utilizing the materials —all geared to get children to think about, react, to, and appreciate poetry.

The recordings are equally good. Narrations are well-paced and banded so that the teacher can pick, choose, and easily find particular selections. The sets are excellent and highly recommended. The aim is to utilize both sound and sight to foster children's interest about poets and poetry. In Group 2, for example, one print is entitled "Towers to the Sky." The large print features construction workers busily putting up a new skyscraper and can spark a good discussion. The reverse side offers a brief introduction about people who watch buildings going up, jokingly called "sidewalk superintendents." The introduction ends with the statement, ". . . a look at our picture may be sufficient to inspire you to write your own poems." Selected poems include "Skyscraper Song" by Thane Gower Ritalin, "Summon of the Workers" by Clara Lambert, "Building a Skyscraper" by James S. Tippett, and "I Hear America Singing" by Walt Whitman.

Students looking at the print can listen to the teacher or another classmate read one or several of the poems, and then he can listen to the recording. From this they might be inspired to create their own poems and/or seek additional poems to enlarge the scope of the theme.

The materials can be used to correlate with language arts and social studies units as well as remedial reading, listening skills, and art. Each set is enclosed in a sturdy, plastic folder.

171

CHILDREN AS PRODUCERS

There is great emphasis today on encouraging elementary school children to produce their own recordings, films, and filmstrips. Poetry is an excellent area in which to spark media-minded boys and girls.

Recordings of poetry can be made in an endless variety of ways via tape or cassette recorders. Tapes can also be made and used to narrate films and filmstrips. In recent years several articles and books have related how teachers have helped children produce such media.

FILMS

Winifred M. Thoren, a media specialist at the East Ridge Elementary School in Lincoln, Nebraska, reports how she involved a kindergarten class in producing an 8mm film, "Apollo 8 Moon Flight," in "Kindergartners Make a Space Film" (*The Instructor,* February 1970, pp. 58–9).

Make Yor Own Animated Movies (Little-Brown, 1970) by Yvonne Anderson and *Children as Film Makers* (Van Nostrand Reinhold, 1970) by John Lidstone and Dan McIntosh are two excellent resources. *Make Your Own Animated Movies* tells of the Yellow Ball Workshop in Lexington, Massachusetts, and how, since 1963, children ranging in ages from five to nineteen have been producing cartoons. The text, written by the Workshop's director, describes how children or adults working with children can create successful animated films. *Children as Film Makers* relates just about all there is to know about filmmaking, from selecting a camera to creating film presentations. A fine bibliography is included to guide you even further along. The text's premise is "children can make films—good films—on their own, from beginning to end."

Filmmaking for Children (Pflaum/Standard, 1971) by Arden Rynew is another fine handbook. The author, a filmmaker and art teacher, presents a detailed yet usable approach to teaching children the art of producing media. The teacher edition of this paperbound text contains four chapters: "Background," "The Implementation of a Filmmaking Program," "Additional Filmmaking Information," and "Motion Picture Production Handbook," which includes a glossary of terms. The teacher edition of *Filmmaking for Children,* which also contains the student handbook, is available for $3.95; the student edition alone is $1.65.

Terry Barker reports on a "Filming Poetry" project conducted at the Max Cameron High School in British Columbia, Canada, with tenth-grade students (*Scholastic Teacher,* secondary edition, April 5, 1971, pp. 10–11). His project took approximately five to six weeks; the class ended up with an eighteen-minute film consisting of ten visualized poems chosen by the students and a sound track recorded during class sessions. The article includes a discussion of five resources necessary for such a class project.

Another resource to consult is *Media and Methods* magazine, November 1969; this entire issue is devoted to films and filmmaking. You can also send for two free helpful brochures: *Movies with a Purpose* and *Outline for Teaching a Course in Basic Movie-Making,* available from Eastman Kodak Company, Rochester, New York 14650.

With the availability of inexpensive equipment and guides such as the above, any elementary class can surely become involved in producing poetry films.

Children can gain a great deal of knowledge and insight into media production by creating their own filmstrips. The following resources will help you and your class get started.

In "We Make Filmstrips—So Can You!" (*The Instructor,* March, 1967, pp. 44–5), Mary Lou Alsen, a first-grade teacher in Oceanside, California, relates how she used a 35mm camera with her class to produce an inexpensive filmstrip relating to economics.

Dwight R. Wilhelm's article, "Our Group Wants to Make a Filmstrip" (*Audiovisual Instruction,* April 1968, pp. 366–7), explores matters to consider before starting to produce filmstrips.

Doris P. Miller cites a clear and practical list of nineteen dos and don'ts when making filmstrips in "Adventure in Educational Media: Making Sound Filmstrips" (*English Journal,* February 1968, pp. 223–7).

The New York Times Book and Educational Division has available a filmstrip-recording set, *Interpretations: The Me Nobody Knows,* which was constructed from beginning to end by a sixth-grade class. The filmstrip was made by eleven-year-olds in Yorktown Heights, New York, a suburban community, after they reacted to a series of poems written by children "from a black ghetto" and collected in Stephen M. Josephs' widely acclaimed book, *The Me Nobody Knows: Children's Voices from the Ghetto* (Avon, 1969). On side 1, band 1, of the record is an introduction for teachers underscoring certain aspects of the children's work. A pamphlet is enclosed in the kit giving specific directions for making a sound filmstrip.

Hudson Photographic Industries, Inc. has produced an exciting kit, *Multi-Media Learning Materials* (distributed by Miller-Brody Productions, Inc.). It is designed to let girls and boys create their own simple filmstrips and contains twenty-five feet of "U" film (blank filmstrip), ten empty filmstrip cans with blank labels, a set of color markers, a filmstrip splicer block, filmstrip slice tape, a cutting blade, and a teachers' guide. Children can make illustrations on the "U" film with felt-tip pens, pencils, or ballpoint pens; script can be applied with a typewriter. The film is standard 35mm that fits standard projectors; the material can be erased and re-used. Replacement parts are also available at a moderate cost.

Scholastic's *"Draw Your Own Filmstrip and Slide Kit"* contains twenty-five feet of film, over two feet of clear film for slide-making activities, twenty 35mm slide mounts, ten special pencils in assorted colors, ten plastic filmstrip containers for storing completed filmstrips, ten blank filmstrip identification labels, and a set of easy-to-follow instructions. The kit comes in a specially constructed carrying case.

A BRIEF AFTERWORD

In A. A. Milne's delightful classic *The House at Pooh Corner* (Dutton, 1928), the renowned Winnie-the-Pooh sums up the creation of poetry in one line. He tells his friend Piglet, "It is the best way to write poetry, letting things come."

Letting things come is the way of poetry, for poetry can help life along no matter what age or stage of development we are at:

> Poetry can—
>
> Make you chuckle,
> or laugh, or cry,
> make you dance
> or shout, or sigh.

Why? Because poetry, like life, comes about naturally. For each step we take, each decade we live, poetry can weave—

> in and out
> and
> up and down
> and
> around and around
> us—just like life itself.

Letting things come, letting poetry come into the lives of children is one of the best things any of us can do as teachers. And we can help by taking the poetic advice of Beatrice Schenk de Regniers when she tells us to:

Keep a Poem in Your Pocket

Keep a poem in your pocket
and a picture in your head
and you'll never feel lonely
at night when you're in bed.

The little poem will sing to you
the little picture bring to you
a dozen dreams to dance to you
at night when you're in bed.

So—
Keep a picture in your pocket
and a poem in your head
and you'll never feel lonely
at night when you're in bed.

Keep a poem in your pocket—or pocketbook, or briefcase, or shopping bag. Pull it out when needed or wanted and spread it around freely. In short, pass the poetry—please!

From the book *Winnie-the-Pooh* by A. A. Milne. Decorations by E. H. Shepard. Copyright, 1926, by E. P. Dutton & Co., Inc. Renewal, 1954, by A. A. Milne. Published by E. P. Dutton & Co., Inc. and used with their permission.

APPENDIX I:
POETRY IN PAPERBACK:
A SELECTED LIST

FOR YOUNG READERS

*Aldis, Dorothy. *The Secret Place and Other Poems*. Scholastic Book Services.

*Bissett, Donald J., ed. *Poetry and Verse for Urban Children*, 3 vols.:
1. *Poems and Verses to Begin On*; 2. *Poems and Verses about Animals*; 3. *Poems and Verses about the City*. San Francisco: Chandler Publishing Company, 1968.

Brown, Margaret Wise. *Where Have You Been?* New York: Scholastic Book Services.
These charming, simple six-lined verses about familiar birds and animals are sure to captivate the very young child's fancy. Illustrations are done by Caldecott Award-winning artist Barbara Cooney.

*Clifton, Lucille. *Everett Anderson's Christmas Coming*. New York: Holt.

*———*Some of the Days of Everett Anderson*. New York: Holt.

Cole, William, comp. *Oh, What Nonsense!* New York: Viking.
Fifty selections of counting rhymes, jump-rope rhymes, and song lyrics are included in this witty anthology. The volume is illustrated by Tomi Ungerer.

———*What's Good for a Four-Year-Old?, What's Good for a Five-Year-Old?, What's Good for a Six-Year-Old?* New York: Holt.
Mr. Cole, the noted anthologist, turns poet in these three books of verse which each year-old will enjoy reading. *Four* is illustrated by Tomi Ungerer; *Five* by Edward Sorel; *Six* by Ingrid Fetz—and each is equally charming.

de Regniers, Beatrice, et al. *Poems Children Will Sit Still For: A Selection for Primary Grades*. New York: Citation Press.
The 106 poems in this volume have been selected to meet primary grade children's interests and experiences. Sections include: "Mostly Weather," "Mostly People," and "Seeing, Feeling, and Thinking." For many of the poems suggestions are offered for reading, for audience participation, or for possible discussion.

---

*Titles marked with an asterisk are discussed within the text of this volume.

*Gross, Ruth Belov. *The Laugh Book*. New York: Scholastic Book Services.

*Hopkins, Lee Bennett. *This Street's for Me!* New York: Scholastic Book Services.

*Issa, Yayū, Kikaku et al. *Don't Tell the Scarecrow and Other Japanese Poems*. New York: Scholastic Book Services.

Jacobs, Leland B. *Alphabet of Girls*. New York: Holt.
This delightful alphabet book goes from Arabella, Araminta, Audrey, and Ann to Zepha and Zelda. The rhymes are complimented by John E. Johnson's two-color illustrations.

————*Is Somewhere Always Far Away?* New York: Holt.
These delightful poems, written by a nationally recognized authority on children's literature, will have special appeal to very young boys and girls. The text is illustrated by John E. Johnson.

Larrick, Nancy, ed. *Piping Down the Valleys Wild*. New York: Dell.
Dr. Larrick knows poetry and knows what children like. This anthology, divided into sixteen sections, includes poems about the weather, animals, people, city, and country. Poets range from A. A. Milne to Gwendolyn Brooks.

Lear, Edward. *A Was Once an Apple Pie*. New York: Scholastic Book Services.
A zesty, rollicking treatment of Lear's classic alphabet. Illustrations are by William Hogarth.

*McCord, David. *Far and Few*. New York: Dell.

McGovern, Ann. *Black Is Beautiful*. New York: Scholastic Book Services.
Illustrated with photographs by Hope Wurmfeld, this poem tells of the many positive things that the color black signifies.

*Moore, Lilian. *I Feel the Same Way*. New York: Scholastic Book Services.

*Sendak, Maurice. *Chicken Soup with Rice*. New York: Scholastic Book Services.

*Wadsworth, Olive A. *Over in the Meadow*. New York: Scholastic Book Services.

Wildsmith, Brian. *Selections from Brian Wildsmith's Mother Goose*. New York: Scholastic Book Services.
Brilliantly colored, highly original illustrations by England's prize-

winning artist. Carefully selected rhymes make this a collection children will treasure.

*Withers, Carl, comp. *Favorite Rhymes from A Rocket in My Pocket.* New York: Scholastic Book Services.

FOR OLDER READERS

*Baron, Virginia Olsen, ed. *Here I Am!: An Anthology of Poems by Young People in Some of America's Minority Groups.* New York: Bantam.

*Benig, Irving, ed. *The Children: Poems and Prose from Bedford Stuyvesant.* New York: Grove Press.

Cornish, Sam, and Lucian W. Dixon, eds. *Chicory: Young Voices from the Black Ghetto.* New York: Association Press.
Poems overheard or written by children in Baltimore, Maryland, all of which have been taken from *Chicory,* a magazine of poetry, fiction, and commentary issued by the Enoch Pratt Free Library's Inner-city Community Action Program.

Clymer, Eleanor, ed. *Arrow Book of Funny Poems.* New York: Scholastic Book Services.
Light verse by such poets and humorists as Edward Lear and Lewis Carroll. A book-record combination featuring selections from the book is also available.

*Crume, Vic, and Gladys Schwarcz, eds. *The Haunted House and Other Spooky Poems and Tales.* New York: Scholastic Book Services.

*de Gasztold, Carmen Bernos, trans. by Rumer Godden. *The Creature's Choir.* New York: Viking.

————*Prayers from the Ark.* New York: Viking.

*Hopkins, Lee Bennett, and Misha Arenstein, comps. *Faces and Places: Poems for You.* New York: Scholastic Book Services.

Johnson, James Welden. *God's Trombones.* New York: Viking.
This volume features seven "Negro Sermons in Verse" and contains one of the poet's most famous works, "The Creation."

*Knudson, R. R., and P. K. Ebert. *Sports Poems.* New York: Dell.

*McGovern, Ann, ed. *Arrow Book of Poetry*. New York: Scholastic Book Services.

*Sandburg, Carl. *Wind Song*. New York: Harcourt.

Summerfield, Geoffrey, ed. *First Voices*, 4 vols. New York: Random House. For upper-grade readers this set of four lively, colorful anthologies is a must. The careful balance of poetry and black and white and full-color photographs will spark all kinds of creative activities in the classroom. The poetry ranges from children's writings to just about every major poet you can think of. Book 1 contains eighty poems, thirty pictures; Book 2, eighty-three poems, thirty-one pictures; Book 3, one hundred and eight poems, thirty-six pictures; Book 4, ninety-two poems, thirty-six pictures. A handbook is also available to guide the teacher through all four volumes.

*Weiner, Florence, comp. *Peace Is You and Me: Children's Writings and Paintings on Love and Peace*. New York: Avon.

FOR MATURE READERS

*Adoff, Arnold, comp. *City in All Directions: An Anthology of Modern Poems*. New York: Macmillan.

*————*I Am the Darker Brother: An Anthology of Modern Poems by Black Americans*. New York: Macmillan.

*————*It Is the Poem Singing into Your Eyes*. New York: Harper.

Bettenbender, John, ed., *Poetry Festival*. New York: Dell.
A compilation of verse containing over 150 of the most popular poems in the English language. The book is "designed primarily for young readers who have yet to discover the pleasure of these old favorites..." There are twelve sections as well as biographical notes.

Dunning, Stephen, ed. *Mad, Sad and Glad*. New York: Scholastic Book Services. See annotation in Appendix II.

*Larrick, Nancy. *I Heard a Scream in the Street*. New York: Bantam.

*————*On City Streets*. New York: Bantam.

*Jordan, June, ed. *Soulscript: Afro-American Poetry*. New York: Doubleday.

*————and Terri Bush, comps. *The Voice of the Children*. New York: Holt.

*Joseph, Stephen M., ed. *The Me Nobody Knows.* New York: Avon.

McGinley, Phyllis. *Times Three.* New York: Viking.
>A selection of 300 poems of the poet's best work from three decades. The poet is winner of the 1961 Pulitzer Prize for Poetry. This book is definitely for the mature reader in the upper grades.

Molloy, Paul, ed. *100 Plus American Poems.* New York: Scholastic Book Services.
>Over a hundred poems comprise this fine collection. The book is illustrated with black and white photographs selected from the annual Scholastic/Kodak Photography Awards.

*Peck, Richard, comp. *Sounds and Silences.* New York: Dell.

Swenson, May. *Poems to Solve.* New York: Scribner.
>There are poems to solve in each of the poet's works. In her introduction, "A Clue or Two," Miss Swenson states: "These poems were selected with the aim of presenting the direct experience of finding and recognizing, comparing and contrasting, shaping and naming, solving and enjoying—thus inviting the reader to share with the poet some of the primary pleasures of the creative act itself."

APPENDIX II:
OUTSTANDING VOLUMES OF POETRY
WRITTEN BY CHILDREN FOR
CHILDREN: A SELECTED LIST

With the exception of *Mad, Sad and Glad,* and *Chicory,* all these titles are discussed within the text of this volume:

Adoff, Arnold. *It Is the Poem Singing into Your Eyes.* New York: Harper, 1971; also available in paperback from the publisher.

Baron, Virginia Olsen, ed. *Here I Am!: An Anthology of Poems Written by Young People in Some of America's Minority Groups.* New York: E. P. Dutton, 1969; also available in paperback from Bantam.

Barnstone, Aliki. *The Real Tin Flower: Poems about the World at Nine.* New York: Crowell-Collier, 1968.

Cavin, Tony. *The Bright Red Porcupine.* New York: Harlin Quist, 1969.

Cornish, Sam, and Lucian W. Dixon, eds. *Chicory: Young Voices from the Black Ghetto.* New York: Association Press.
See annotation in Appendix I

Dunning, Stephen, ed. *Mad, Sad and Glad.* New York: Scholastic Book Services, 1971.
Since 1925 Scholastic Magazines has conducted annual creative writing contests for students in grades 7–12. The 101 poems in this volume are from the award winners for the years 1966–1970. The book is illustrated with striking black and white photographs selected from the 1970 Scholastic/Kodak Photography Awards. The text is for mature readers, but the poems reveal a good deal of insight into the world and its problems as expressed through the pens of children across the country.

Hopkins, Lee Bennett, comp. *City Talk.* New York: Alfred A. Knopf, 1970.

Jordon, June, and Terri Bush, eds. *The Voice of the Children.* New York: Holt, 1970; also available in paperback from the publisher.

Larrick, Nancy, ed. *Green Is Like a Meadow of Grass: An Anthology of Children's Pleasure in Poetry.* Champaign, Ill., Garrard, 1968.

————*I Heard a Scream in the Streets.* New York: M. Evans, 1970.

Lewis, Richard, comp. *Miracles: Poems by Children of the English-speaking World.* New York: Simon and Schuster, 1966.

————*The Wind and the Rain: Children's Poems.* New York: Simon and Schuster, 1968.

Schaefer, Charles E., and Kathleen C. Miller, eds. *Young Voices.* New York: Bruce Publishing Co., 1971.

APPENDIX III:
SOURCES OF EDUCATIONAL
MATERIALS CITED

American Heritage Publishing Company, Inc., 551 Fifth Ave., New York,
N. Y. 10017

Association Press, 291 Broadway, New York, N. Y. 10007

Atheneum Publishers, 122 East 42nd St., New York, N. Y. 10017

Avon Books, 959 Eighth Ave., New York, N. Y. 10019

Bantam Books, Inc., 666 Fifth Ave., New York, N. Y. 10019

Bobbs-Merrill, Inc., 4300 West 62nd St., Indianapolis, Ind. 46268

Bowmar, 622 Rodier Drive, Glendale, Calif. 91201

Chandler Publishing Company, 124 Spear St., San Francisco, Calif. 94105

Citation Press, 50 West 44th St., New York, N. Y. 10036

Coronet Films, 65 East South Water St., Chicago, Ill. 60601

Crowell (Thomas Y.) Company, 600 Fifth Ave., New York, N.Y. 10022

Crowell Collier & MacMillan, Inc., 866 Third Ave., New York, N. Y. 10022

Crown Publishers, Inc., 419 Park Ave. South, New York, N. Y. 10016

Day (John) Company, Inc., 257 Park Ave., New York, N. Y. 10010

Delacorte Press, 750 Third Ave., New York, N. Y. 10017

Dell Publishing Company, Inc., 750 Third Ave., New York, N. Y. 10017

Dial Press, Inc., 750 Third Ave., New York, N. Y. 10017

Dodd, Mead & Company, Inc., 79 Madison Ave., New York, N. Y. 10016

Doubleday and Company, Inc., 277 Park Ave., New York, N. Y. 10017

Dover Publications, 180 Varick St., New York, N. Y. 10014

Dutton (E. P.) & Company, 201 Park Ave. South, New York, N. Y. 10003

Evans (M.) & Co., Inc., 216 West 49th St., New York, N. Y. 10017

Farrar, Straus & Giroux, Inc., 19 Union Square West, New York, N. Y.
10003

Folkways/Scholastic Records, 50 West 44th St., New York, N. Y. 10036

Four Winds Press, 50 West 44th St., New York, N. Y. 10036

Gale Research, Book Tower, Detroit, Mich. 48226

Garrard Publishing Co., 1607 North Market St., Champaign, Ill. 61820

Grove Press, Inc., 53 East 11th St., New York, N. Y. 10003

Harcourt, Brace, Jovanovich, 757 Third Ave., New York, N. Y. 10017

Harper & Row, Publishers, 10 East 53rd St., New York, N. Y. 10022

Heath (D. C.) and Company, 125 Spring St., Lexington, Mass. 02173

Holt, Rinehart and Winston, Inc., 383 Madison Ave., New York, N. Y. 10017

Houghton Mifflin Co., 2 Park St., Boston, Mass. 02107

Hubbard Press, 2855 Shermer Rd., Northbrook, Ill. 60062

Knopf (Alfred A.), 201 East 50th St., New York, N. Y. 10022

Lippincott (J. B.) Co., East Washington Sq., Philadelphia, Pa. 19105

Little, Brown & Co., Inc., 34 Beacon St., Boston, Mass. 02106

Lothrop, Lee and Shepard Co., Inc., 105 Madison Ave., New York, N. Y. 10016

Loyola University Press, 3441 North Ashland Ave., Chicago, Ill. 60657

McCall Books, 230 Park Ave., New York, N. Y. 10017

Macmillan Co., 866 Third Ave., New York, N. Y. 10022

McGraw-Hill Book Company, 330 West 42nd St., New York, N. Y. 10036

Media Plus, 60 Riverside Drive, New York, N. Y. 10024

Meridian Books, World Publishing Company, 110 East 59th St., New York, N. Y. 10022

Miller-Brody Productions, Inc., 342 Madison Ave., New York, N. Y. 10017

National Council of Teachers of English, 1111 Kenyon Road, Urbana, Ill. 61801

New York Times Book and Educational Division, 229 West 43rd St., New York, N. Y. 10036

Pantheon Books, 201 East 50th St., New York, N. Y. 10022

Pflaum (George A.), 38 West Fifth St., Dayton, Ohio 45402

Prentice-Hall, Inc., Englewood Cliffs, N. J. 07632

Putnam's (G. P.) Sons, 200 Madison Ave., New York, N. Y. 10016

Quist Books (Harlin), distributed by Franklin Watts

Rand McNally & Co., Box 7600, Chicago, Ill. 60680

Random House, Inc., 201 East 50th St., New York, N. Y. 10022

Scholastic Book Services, 50 West 44th St., New York, N. Y. 10036

Seabury Press, 815 Second Ave., New York, N. Y. 10017

Scribner's (Charles) Sons, 597 Fifth Ave., New York, N. Y. 10017

Shorewood Reproductions, Inc., 724 Fifth Ave., New York, N. Y. 10019

Simon and Schuster, 630 Fifth Ave., New York, N. Y. 10020

Spoken Arts, Inc., 310 North Ave., New Rochelle, N. Y. 10801

Teachers College Press, Columbia University, 1234 Amsterdam Ave., New York, N. Y. 10027

United States Government Printing Office, Superintendent of Documents, Washington, D. C. 20401

University of Arizona Press, Box 3398, Tucson, Ariz. 85722

Van Nostrand Reinhold, 450 West 33rd St., New York, N. Y. 10001

Viking Press, Inc., 625 Madison Ave., New York, N. Y. 10022

Wagner Printing Co., 2603 San Pablo Ave., Berkeley, Calif. 94702

Watts (Franklin), Inc., 845 Third Ave., New York, N. Y. 10022

Weston Woods, Weston, Conn. 06880

Wilson (H. W.) Co., 950 University Ave., Bronx, N. Y. 10452

AUTHOR INDEX

TITLE INDEX

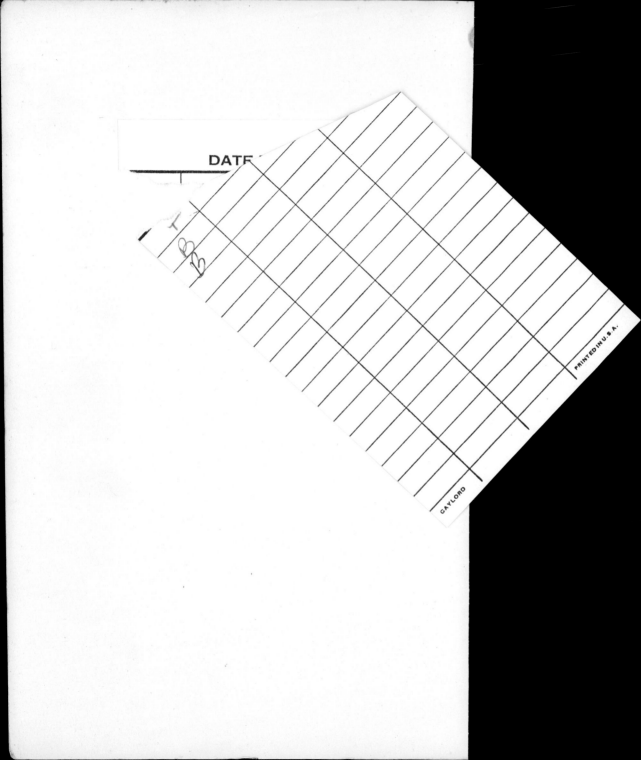

DATE